Text by Rose Houk

THE PEAKS

Photographs by *Arizona Highways* Contributors

1

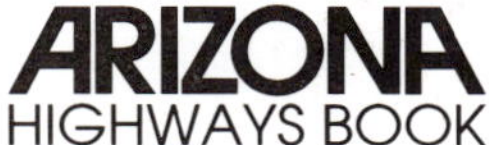

(FRONT COVER) *The elegant profile of the San Francisco Peaks can be seen from all over northern Arizona. The Peaks, the highest mountains in Arizona, rise to 12,643 feet elevation.* PETER BLOOMER

(INSIDE FRONT COVER) *Cool, green ferns carpet aspen forests in northern Arizona at around 8,000 feet.* JOHN DREW

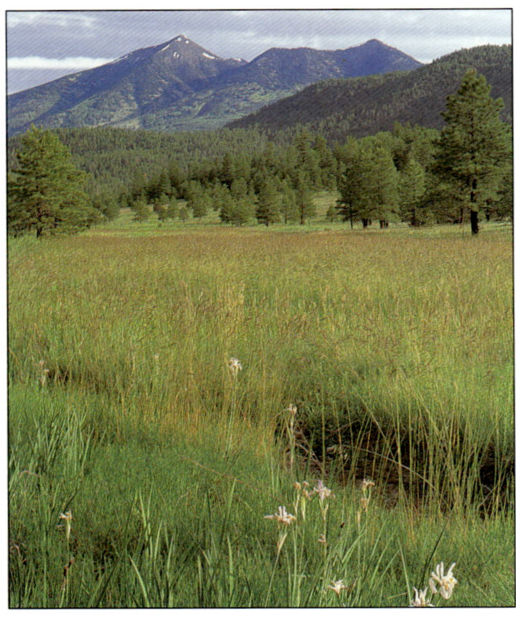

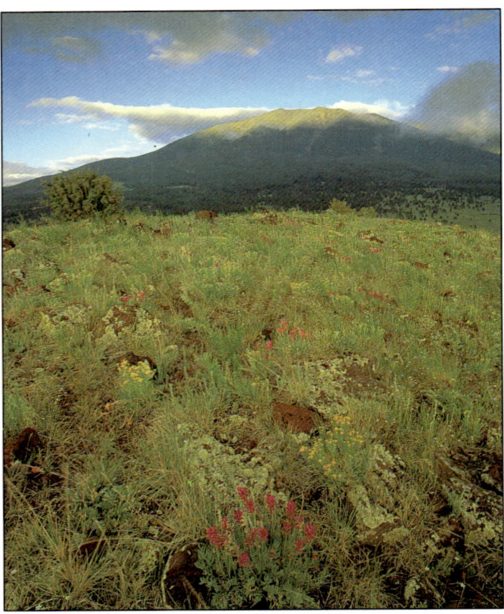

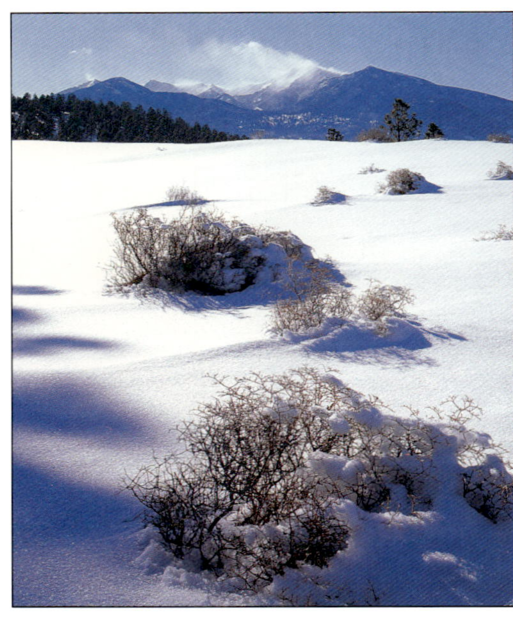

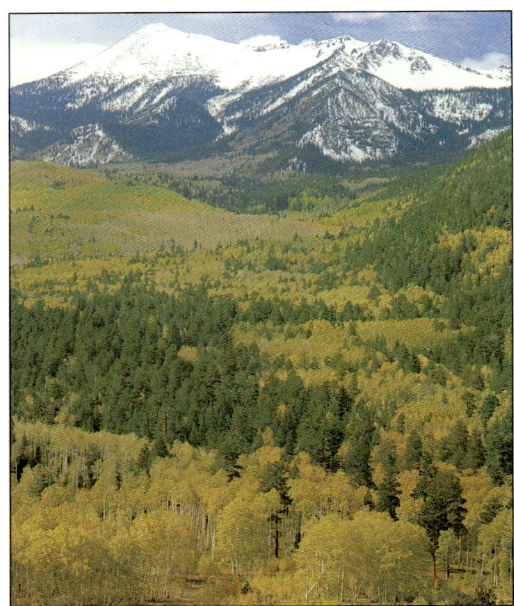

Prepared by the Book Division of *Arizona Highways* magazine, a monthly publication
of the Arizona Department of Transportation.
Hugh Harelson – Publisher / Robert J. Farrell – Book Editor
Peter Ensenberger – Picture Editor / Gary Bennett – Creative Director
Cindy Mackey – Production Director

Library of Congress Number 94–079757
ISBN 0–916179–48–6

CONTENTS

(OPPOSITE PAGE, CLOCKWISE FROM TOP LEFT) *The high country of northern Arizona is a land of four seasons –wild iris grace meadows in spring, colorful wildflowers spangle the land after summer rains, aspens lend their touch of gold in fall, and snow blankets the earth through winter.*
ROBERT McDONALD, TOM BEAN, LARRY ULRICH AND JERRY SIEVE

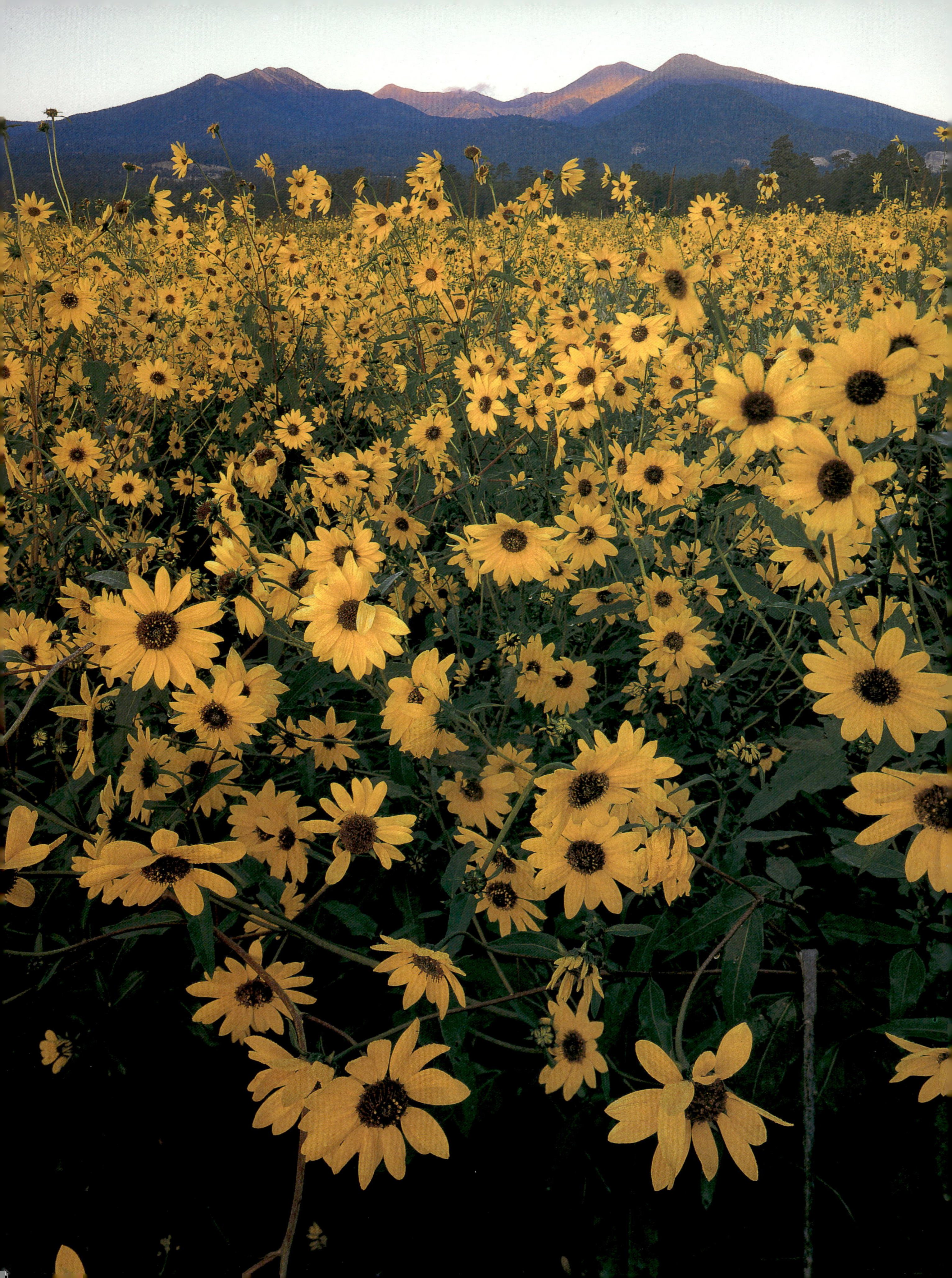

Introduction

Flagstaff, Williams, and Northern Arizona's High Country

I remember my first visit to Flagstaff and northern Arizona. It was springtime. I'd quit my job at a small newspaper in southeast Kentucky, invested part of my savings in a blue canvas tent and a Sears backpack, and headed west with a friend on a once-in-a-lifetime adventure. We were traveling in and camping out of a VW squareback, hoping to be on the road for three months, or for as long as our money held out.

Obviously, the Grand Canyon was on our itinerary. I'll never forget my first sight of the snow-covered San Francisco Peaks suddenly rising to more than 12,000 feet before me on the horizon as I headed north on Interstate 17 from Phoenix. I'm basically a kid from Indiana, and, though I'd just spent some time in the Appalachians, these were my first *real* mountains.

Driving through Flagstaff, I entertained vague thoughts of living in a place like this someday. That was more than 20 years ago. In the interim, I resided in several places, including a couple of years at the Grand Canyon. For me, then, Flagstaff was the big city. I'd ride the Trailways from the Canyon, do whatever shopping I could within walking distance of the bus station, then head back to the Canyon.

I was hooked. It took a while longer before Flagstaff actually became my home. But now it is, for the duration, if all goes well.

(OPPOSITE PAGE) *Beneath the towering backdrop of the San Francisco Peaks, Bonito Park, northeast of Flagstaff, teems with golden sunflowers in late summer.*
JACK DYKINGA

As for so many others, the San Francisco Peaks drew me here, and hold me now. I think I understand some of the reasons the Navajo and Hopi revere them, for I too hold the Peaks in high regard. The mountains' overriding presence captivates and sustains me. Also, there's the forest of ponderosa pine that fills the air with such sweetness and provides refuge within minutes of my home.

Along the climb from the deserts of southern Arizona on Interstate 17, roadside signs tell of the gradual elevation gain — 5,000 feet, then 6,000. Topping the rise that overlooks the red rock country of Oak Creek Canyon to the west, you've almost reached 7,000 feet. This is the magic elevation that marks the beginning of the forest of tall ponderosa pines, which covers a huge swath of northern Arizona. The air takes on an unmistakable clarity and coolness. Signs warn to watch for deer and elk on the roadway.

At this point you've reached the top of the Mogollon Rim, that impressive escarpment that cuts across Arizona's midsection, southeast-to-northwest, the major topographic feature that separates northern Arizona from southern Arizona. So different are these two sections, you may wonder that they belong in the same state.

The Mogollon Rim marks the southern edge of the 130,000-square-mile Colorado Plateau, one of the continent's major geologic provinces. Upon this vast uplift you'll find a seemingly unending landscape that includes Arizona's Grand Canyon, Monument Valley, Canyon de Chelly, and Painted Desert. Atop the rim, you've risen more than one vertical mile above the deserts of central Arizona. The top of the San Francisco Peaks in front of you amounts to a gain of another vertical mile.

Still heading north on I-17, you pass the turnoffs for Munds Park and Kelly Canyon. Old ranches sit in peaceful repose beside big meadows. Dark brown and black volcanic rocks cap cream-colored limestone. Though you've left the desert behind, this is still a dry land. There is an absence of flowing water. Its most common form here is snow, which melts into a series of small lakes south of Flagstaff.

With little notice, you arrive in the bustling town of Flagstaff, the San Francisco Peaks posing majestically north of town. Hub of Arizona's high country, Flagstaff sits almost dead center in the region.

Thirty miles west of Flagstaff, the town of Williams nestles against the base of Bill Williams Mountain. Other high mountains, notably Kendrick and Sitgreaves, rise on the nearby horizon, all of them extinct volcanoes. Calling herself the "Gateway to the Grand Canyon," Williams is the exuberant, smaller sister to Flagstaff with a similar history but with a character all her own. South of Williams, Sycamore Point overlooks Sycamore Canyon Wilderness and a broken, vertiginous drop off the Mogollon Rim. This point defines the southwestern edge of our geography of northern Arizona's high country for this book.

East, and north, beyond Flagstaff, the landscape changes drastically again. With a thousand-foot decrease in elevation, sensuous cinder cones undulate across platinum-grassed plains spotted with stunted piñon and juniper trees. This open, sparsely inhabited region, the San Francisco volcanic field, beckons exploration.

Farther east, the land steps down again to the Little Colorado River, punctuated by Grand Falls, which sometimes flows in a torrent in spring. Big cattle ranches, the Navajo and Hopi Indian lands, and the Painted Desert stretch between and beyond.

This diverse landscape is Peaks country, filled with enough variety and natural attractions to keep any outdoors explorer enthralled for a lifetime.

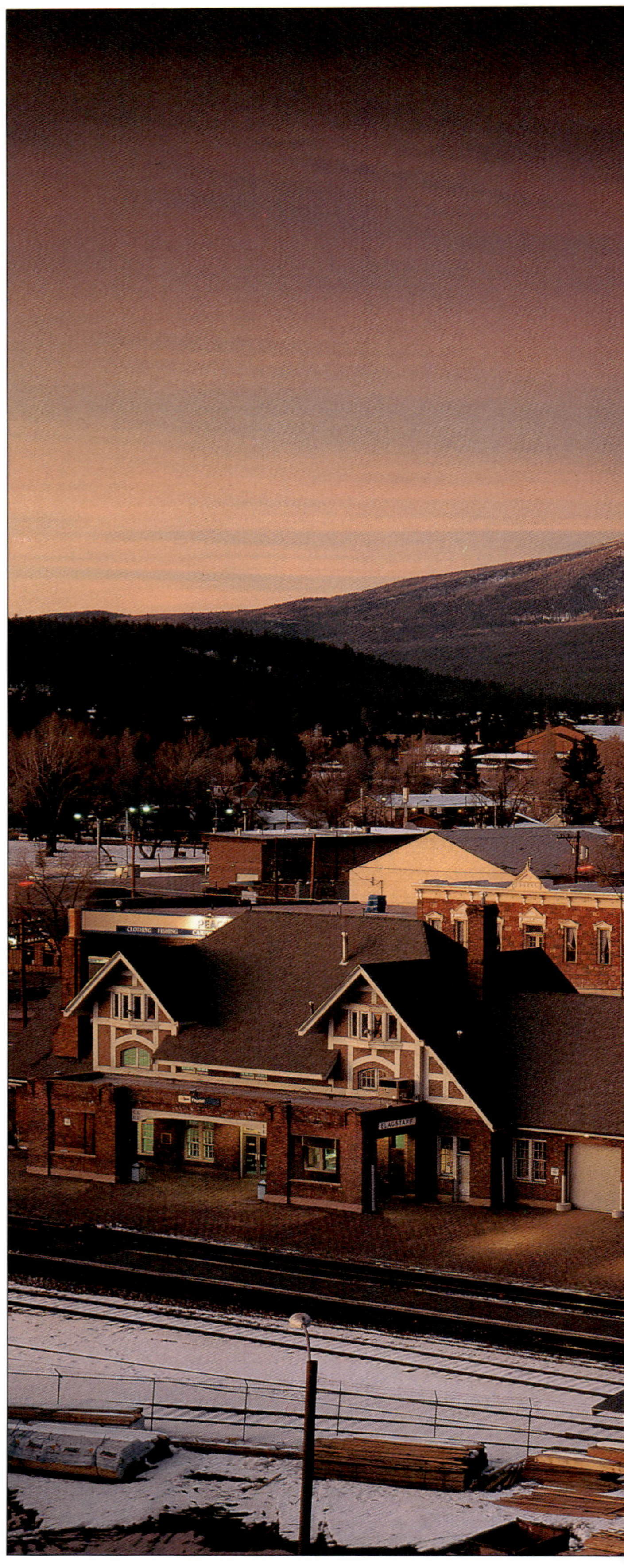

Like a toy railroad town, Flagstaff's historic downtown parallels the Santa Fe Railroad tracks. The San Francisco Peaks are a constant presence anywhere in town.
DAMON BULLOCK

A Flagstaff resident and regular contributor to *Arizona Highways* magazine, **Rose Houk** has written a number of books on a variety of Southwestern subjects, including natural history and archaeology. This is her first book for *Arizona Highways*.

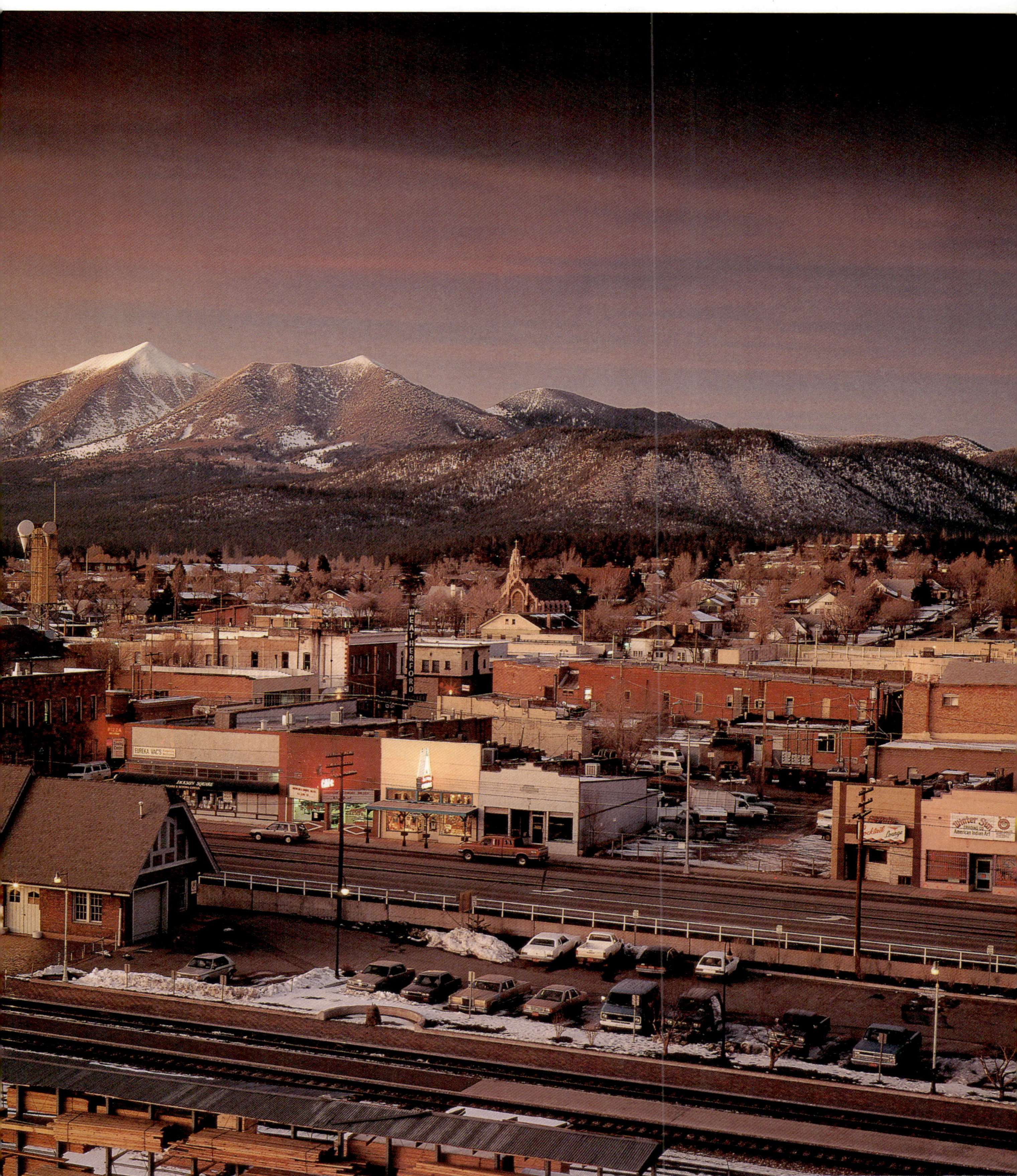
WEATHERFORD
EUREKA VAC'S
Winter Sun
American Indian Art

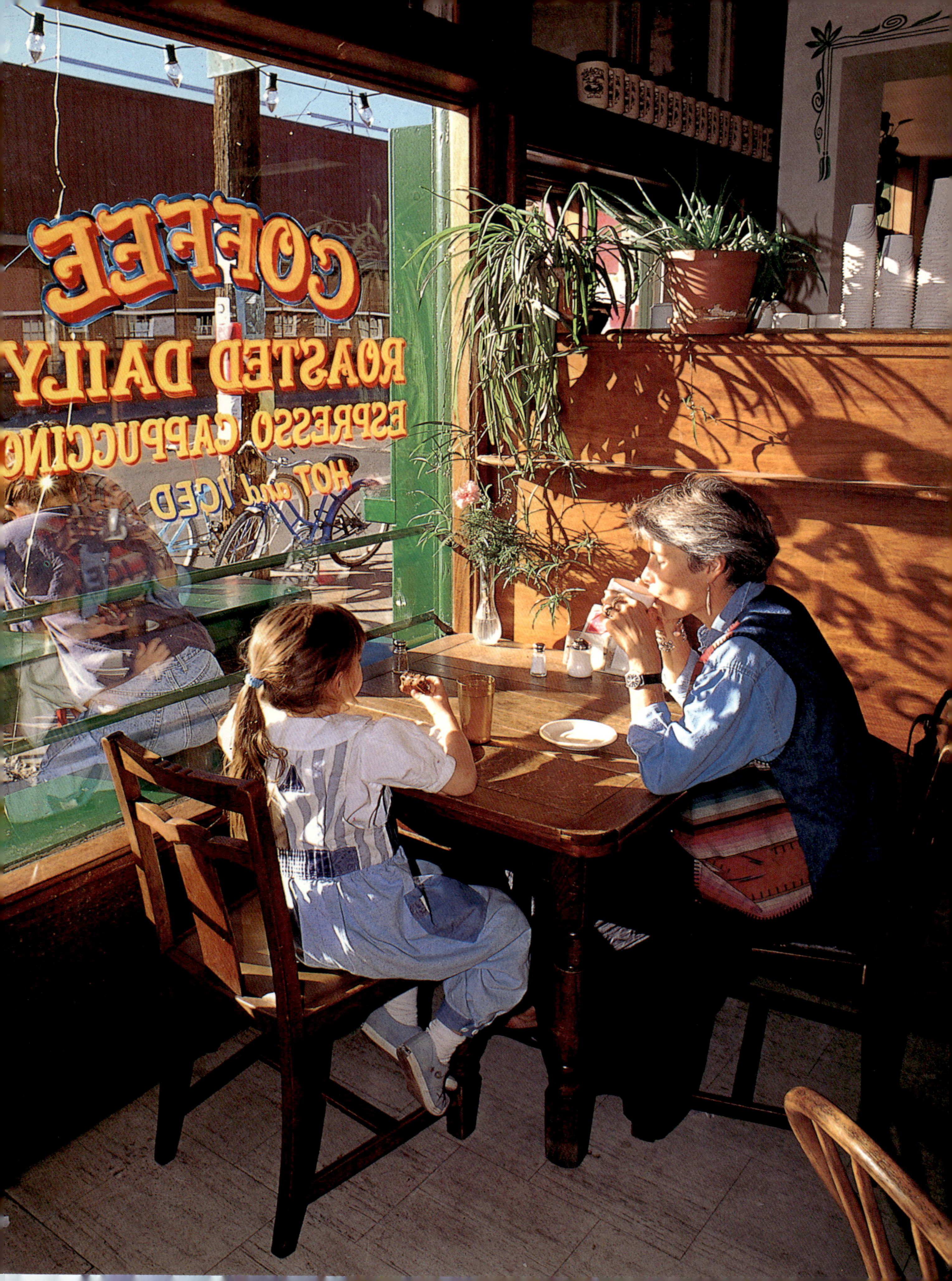
COFFEE
ROASTED DAILY
ESPRESSO CAPPUCCINO
HOT and ICED

Chapter One

FLAGSTAFF

Vibrant City in the Pines Exuding Small-town Charm

On a pine-scented, sun-dappled summer morning, absorbed chess players ponder moves at tables outside Macy's Coffee House on South Beaver Street. Skateboarders weave by, dodging students on mountain bikes. Two dingoes bark from the back of a mud-spattered pickup truck driven by a grizzled cowboy. A Navajo grandmother in velvet blouse and long skirt strolls across an intersection. A Hopi craftsman comes by with a kachina doll for sale. On any day in downtown Flagstaff you're likely to see a kaleidoscopic assortment of people — professionals in suits and ties, cowboys, Indians, European and Asian tourists, skiers, university students, New Agers, and hippie holdouts from the '60s.

Flagstaff harbors a unique mix of people. Blend the tourism industry workforce at the hotels, restaurants, and tour companies with the construction workers, river runners, shopkeepers, lumberjacks, and students, then throw in a disproportionately high number of Ph.D.s — professors and researchers at the university, and astronomers, anthropologists, archaeologists, and paleontologists at various private and governmental scientific facilities — and you pretty much have the picture. Factor this population in with the region's spectacular natural beauty and you begin to understand and appreciate this bustling, youthful, outdoors-oriented hub of northern Arizona.

(OPPOSITE PAGE) *Flagstaff's funky south side is a popular hangout for serious espresso drinkers and others who simply want to be where it's happening.* STEWART AITCHISON
(FOLLOWING PANEL, PAGES 10 AND 11) *The intersection of two major interstates, I-17 and I-40, makes Flagstaff a hub for northern Arizona.* DON B. STEVENSON

"I came in 1970 as a hippie and never left," laughed Elson Miles. It's an oft-heard story in Flagstaff. People come, they stay.

What keeps him here? "The people," answered Miles, without a moment's thought. "And the natural forces . . . like the hellacious south wind I fought all day yesterday."

Miles had just pedaled a one-speed bicycle to Cottonwood, 48 miles away. It was no accident that the bike had only one gear. "I've always been kind of a minimalist," he said as he stood proud and tall beside his bike.

That minimalist streak showed through when Miles, soon after arriving in Flagstaff 25 years ago, started a bicycle shop in a garage on South Beaver Street. He watched his business grow, expanded to a larger store on South San Francisco Street, but always kept his overhead low. In his mid-40s, he wanted something else. He sold his business, went back to school, and now guides bicycle trips.

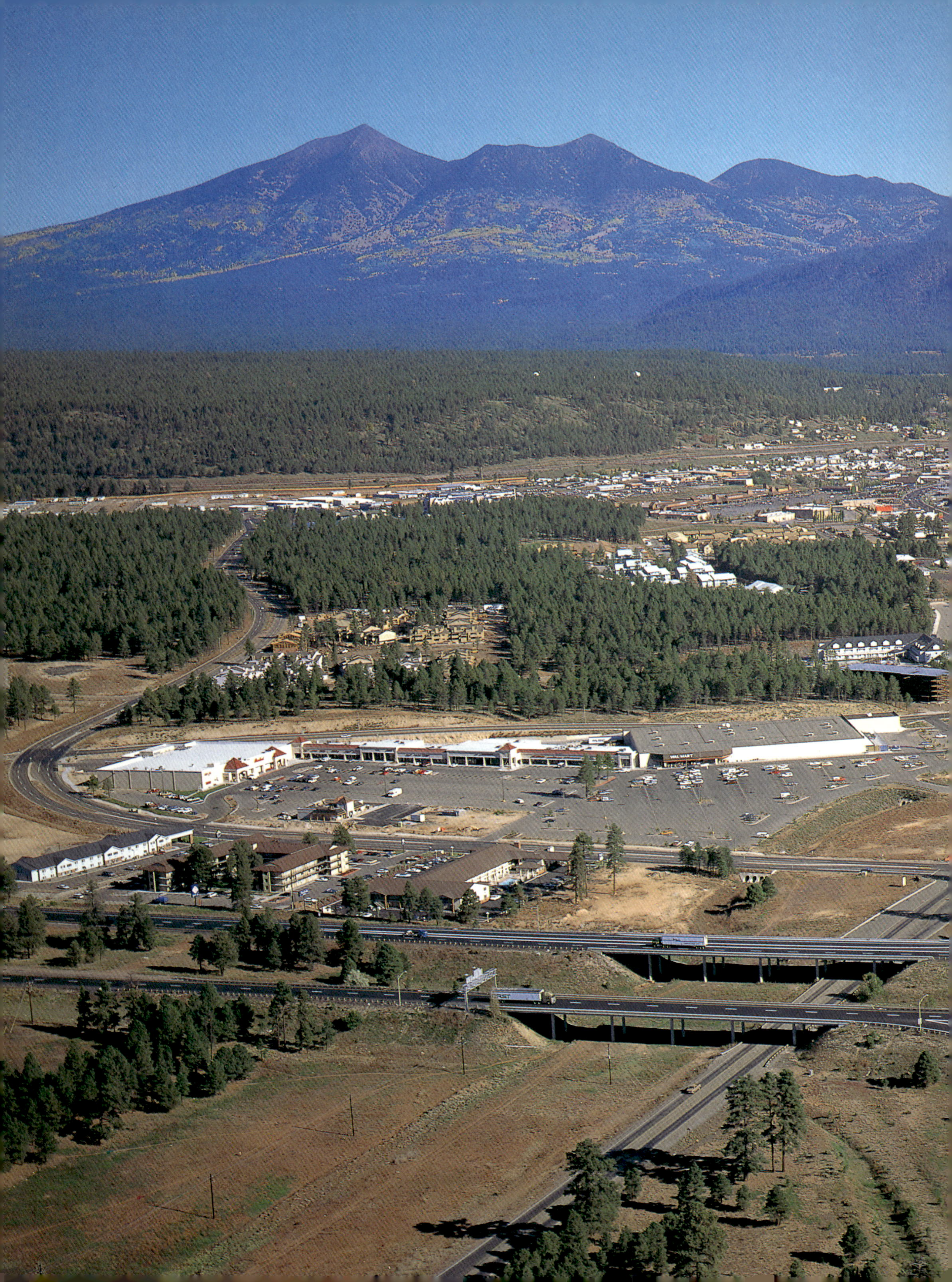

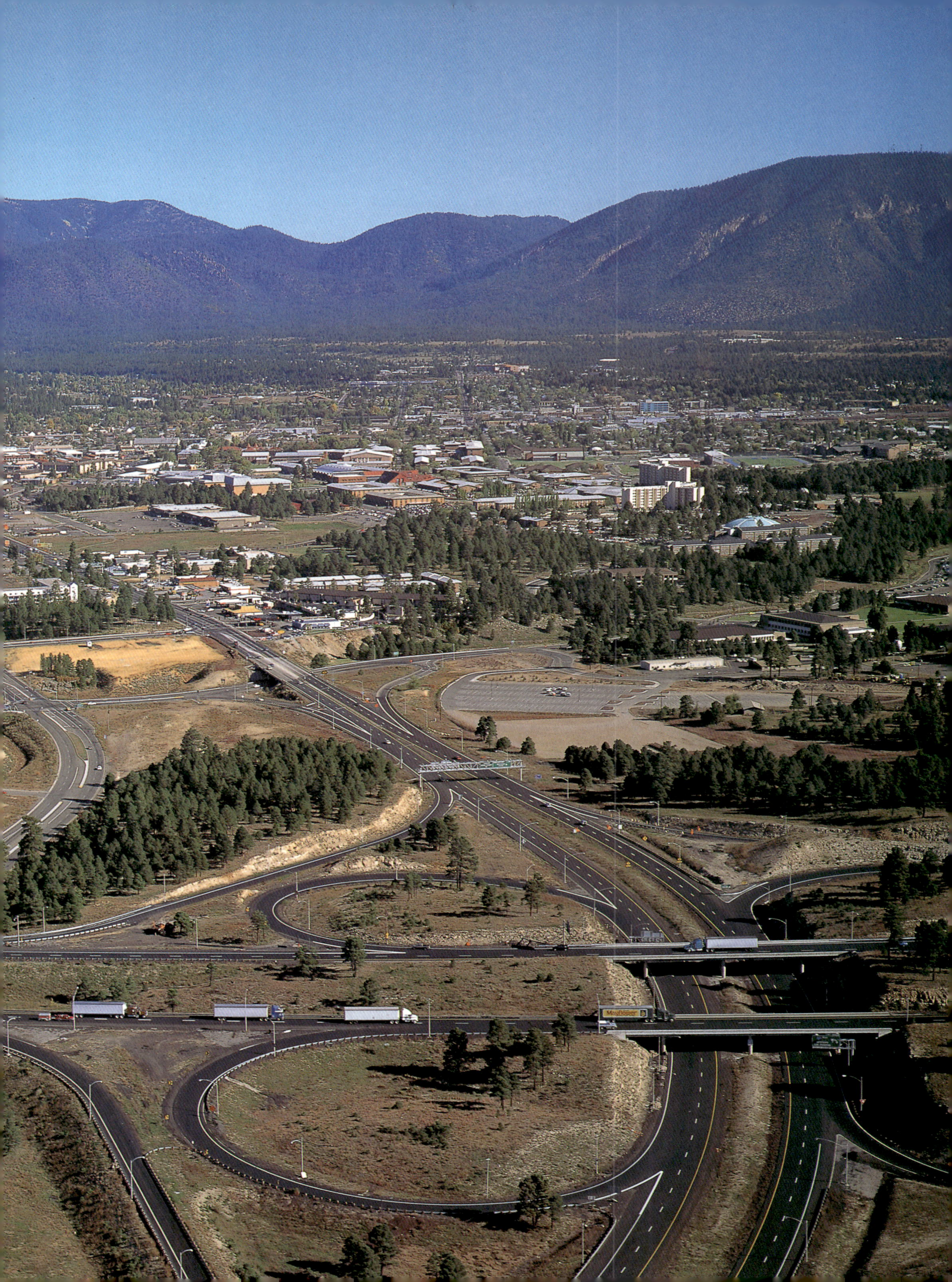

Like many others who have stayed and watched the town grow, Miles is concerned about what Flagstaff will be like for his daughter, Juniper. Now more than twice as large as when Miles moved here, Flagstaff has become a city of nearly 50,000 souls.

Yet Flagstaff still exudes a friendly, small-town atmosphere. At the downtown post office in the morning, people exchange greetings and trade news. Out on the street, the meter maid flashes an irresistible smile as she writes you a parking ticket.

And the town strives to keep the feel of old Flagstaff. Citizens have restored the name of the main drag, Santa Fe Avenue, to Route 66, and several of the "Mother Road's" landmarks still thrive. One of the oldest is the Museum Club, a popular country and western roadhouse with classic neon. Built in 1918 around five living trees, the Museum Club started out life as "the Dean Eldredge Museum and Taxidermist," with displays of stuffed game animals and Indian baskets, pottery, and silver work for sale. It became a roadhouse in 1936, and while the Indian crafts disappeared, the stuffed animals still line the walls and perch on the tree in the bar — hence the nickname "the Zoo Club."

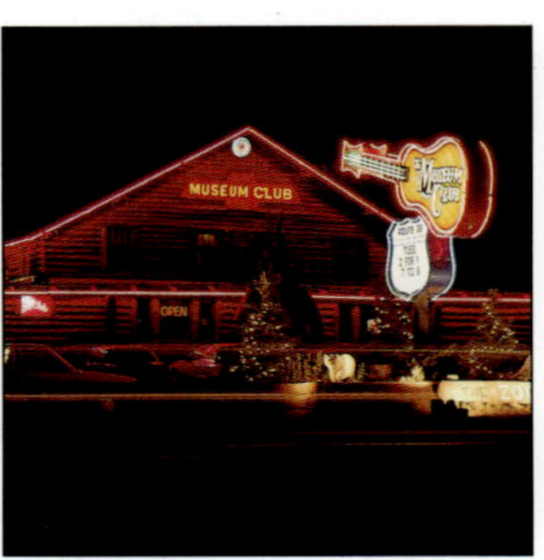

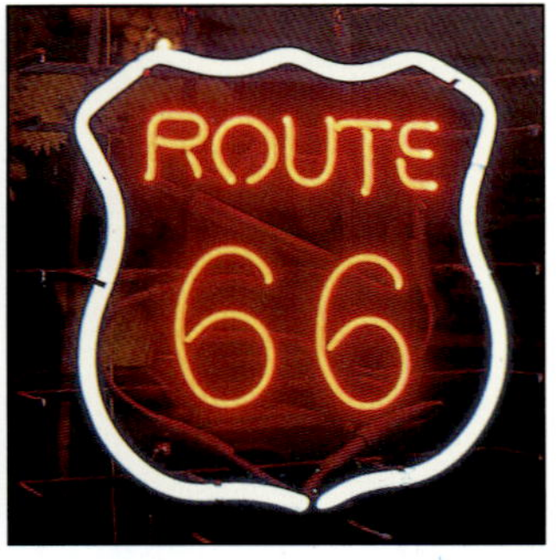

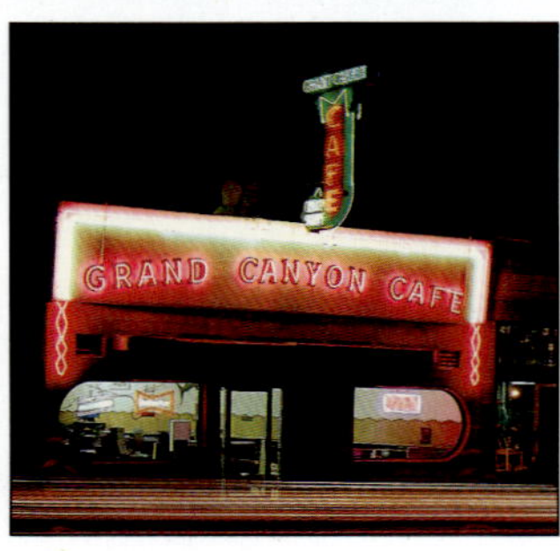

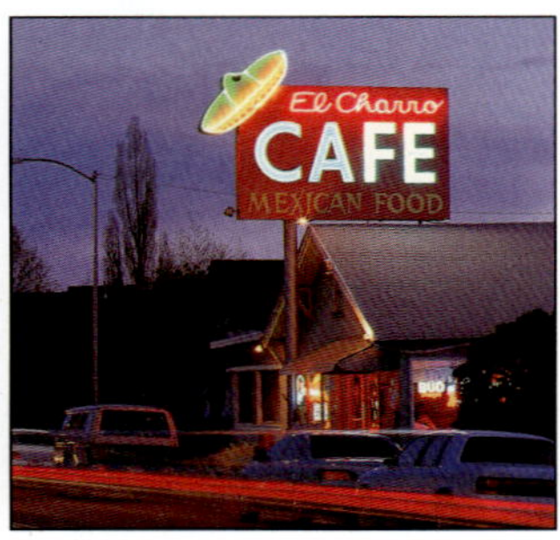

Classic neon glows from Flagstaff's Route 66 landmarks advertising good food and good times.
(ABOVE CLOCKWISE, FROM TOP RIGHT) STEWART AITCHISON, MICHAEL COLLIER, DAMON BULLOCK, MICHAEL COLLIER
(ABOVE RIGHT) *Postal carrier Joseph Vasquez is a familiar daily figure on the streets of downtown Flagstaff.* MICHAEL COLLIER

Some notable Route 66 eateries can still be found, too: the Kachina Cafe for Mexican food; Wong's Grand Canyon Cafe specializing in Chinese food and chicken-fried steak; and Miz Zip's, home of hot apple pie and "Zipburgers." For more than 30 years, Colleen Schutte has baked pies at Miz Zip's. Don't even bother thinking about calories or cholesterol here.

Flagstaff. More an attitude than a town, someone once said. I consider that attitude to be embodied in its people. People like Joseph Vasquez, my mailman. I see him nearly every day, rolling his mail cart along the sidewalks of downtown. He greets me with "*buenos dias*," and I respond in poor Spanish.

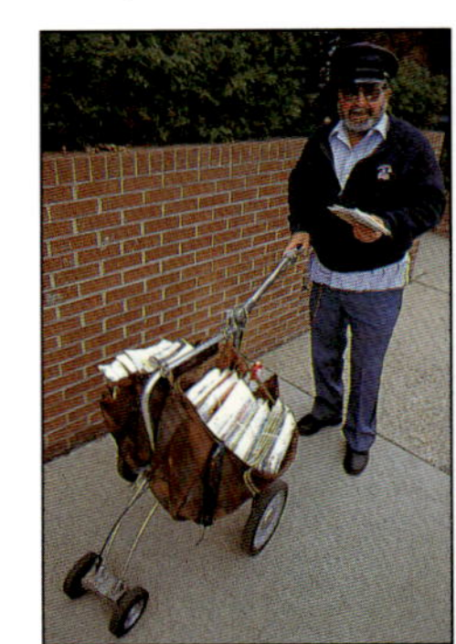

Vasquez and his wife, Mary Lou, are natives of Flagstaff — born and raised here and still living near their families. Vasquez's father, Manuel, came to Flagstaff in 1915 from Mexico with Joseph's great-grandfather, who had escaped the Mexican Revolution. Manuel Vasquez has lived most of his 95 years in the same house on Butler Avenue. Joseph Vasquez remembers his mother, Manuela, selling homemade corn tortillas for 15 cents a dozen in the old days, and his father playing the violin at town dances. Joseph Vasquez has seen many changes in Flagstaff, many newcomers with new ideas. That's good, he says. But his roots run deep and he maintains a strong possessive feeling for his native home: "This is our town," he declares.

If you spend any time at all here, you'll begin to realize why I feel as these people do. Flagstaff's subtle ambiance sneaks up and captivates folks. Before they know it they too begin to cherish the trademark music of the trains that rumble through town, the sweet bells of the Nativity Church, and the cheers from the softball stands that linger late into a summer night.

What drew people to Flagstaff in the beginning were the springs — Leroux, Turkey Tanks, and Elden among them. First, there were Native Americans, followed by Spaniards, New Englanders, African-Americans, and Midwesterners. Later, came hunters, trappers, surveyors, homesteaders, loggers, railroaders, and ranchers, all of whom got word of water through an efficient frontier grapevine. Knowledge of water in the dry land of northern Arizona was priceless.

Leroux Spring, at the base of the San Francisco Peaks, was named for quintessential mountain man and guide Antoine Leroux. His knowledge of the whereabouts of sparkling spring water would eventually lead

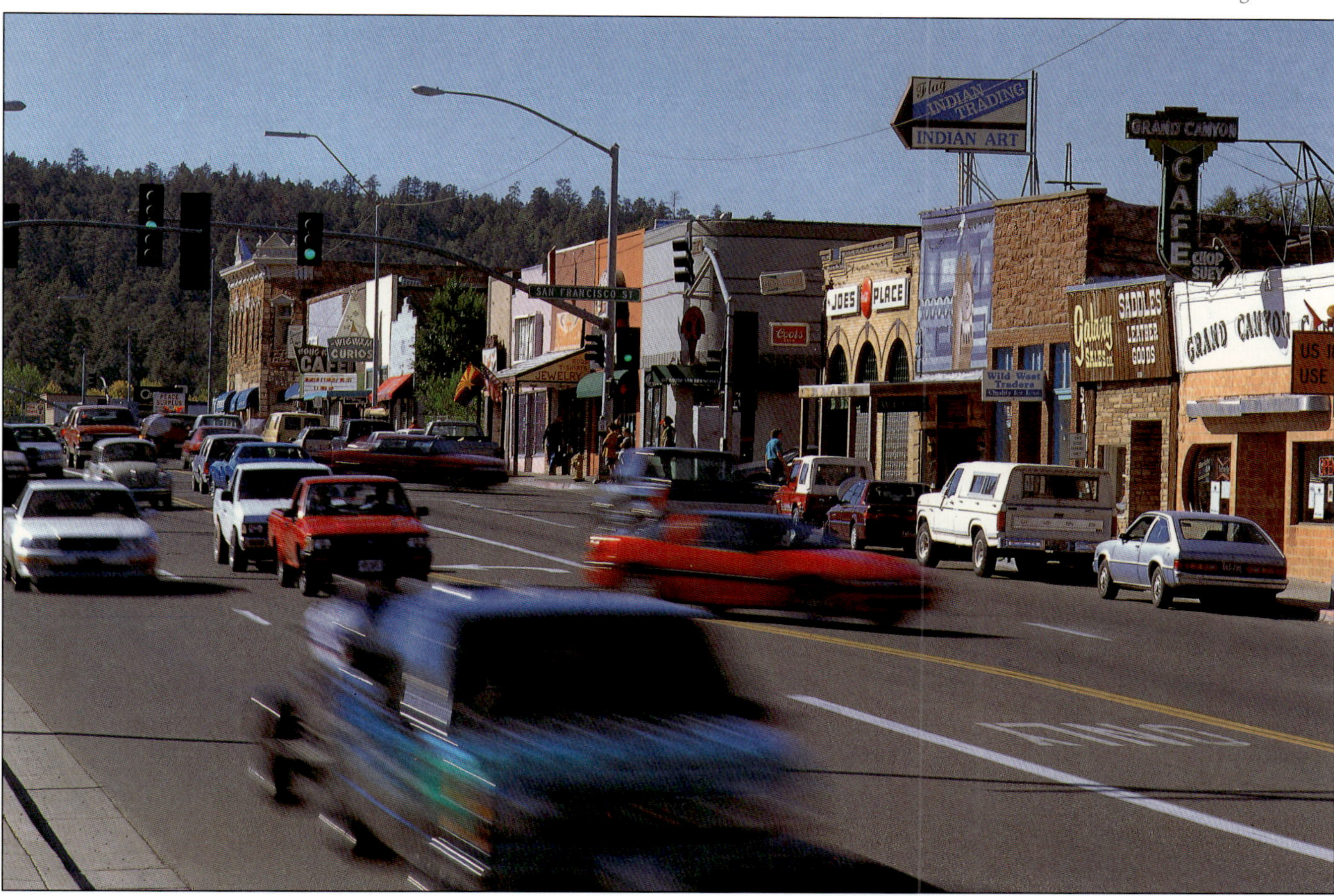

Santa Fe Avenue in Flagstaff has regained its rightful name of Route 66, in honor of the town's heritage. Ever the busy thoroughfare, Route 66 traverses town from east to west. MICHAEL COLLIER

to the birth of Flagstaff.

Lured by overblown descriptions of good farmland in northern Arizona, 50 sons of New England set out from Boston in March 1876. Finding the Little Colorado River valley already spoken for by industrious Mormons, members of the Arizona Colonization Company continued west to Leroux Spring in Fort Valley and started a small settlement there.

Long-standing legend relates that Flagstaff got its name when the Bostonians hoisted a flag up a tall ponderosa pine. History, though, often contains complications: There was not one, but possibly three flag staffs — one at Old Town Spring, another at the foot of Switzer Mesa, and a third raised either by the first Boston group in May 1876, or by a second Boston group on the Fourth of July of the nation's centennial year.

While all three may hold a kernel of truth, journalist and historian Platt Cline believes the town owes its name to the second Boston Party's Fourth of July flag staff. Marked with plaques and a replica pine pole, that historic site is commemorated on the west side of town, near the present Flagstaff junior and senior high schools and Thorpe Park ball fields. By 1878 or 1880, the name "Flag Staff" was appearing in various documents relating to the town.

However the town was named, the fledgling Flagstaff boomed with the arrival of the Atlantic & Pacific Railroad on August 1, 1882, at Old Town Spring, a few miles south of Leroux Spring. Old Man Rumsey (whose first name is lost to history) tried to claim the precious water, spending nights beside the spring. He held a dipper beneath the trickle of water, and when it became heavy he awoke and poured the liquid into a barrel. A barrel of Old Town water, cost 25 cents when the flow was good, but went up to $1.00 when the spring ran low.

Old Town was a lively place. One young man from Iowa thought it high sport to shoot at the railroad construction gangs. Quickly tiring of this, the workers locked the man in a box car. After supper, about 80 of the men prepared to hang the rowdy on the spot, but one faction asked them to show mercy. The railroaders relented and spared him, provided he hightail it back to the Midwest first thing the next morning.

Downtown Flagstaff moved to its present location because the railroad wanted flat land for a depot. Soon after the A&P arrived, railroad officials set up their base of operations a half mile east of Old Town. Quick to spot a trend, merchant P.J. Brannen pulled up stakes at his tent store and moved with them to what soon became known as New Town.

Brannen and others signified their belief in the railroad's economic benefits by erecting permanent stone structures nearby. Brannen's store is still there, with a brick facade, just across Route 66 from the freight depot. It's now Joe's Place, a popular watering hole and pool hall, where, as one local wag has observed, "the elk [stuffed and mounted on the wall] often outnumber the customers."

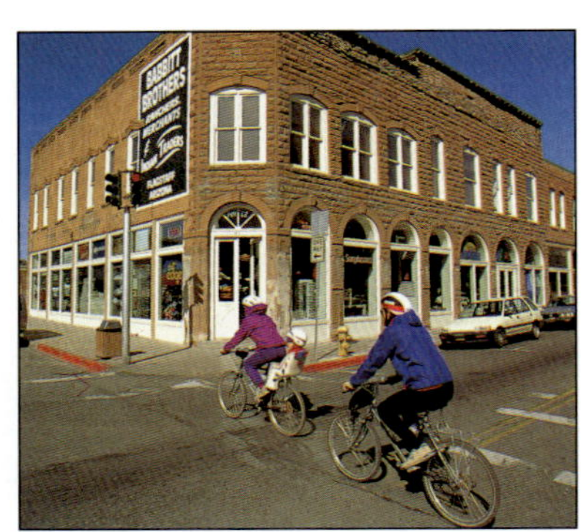

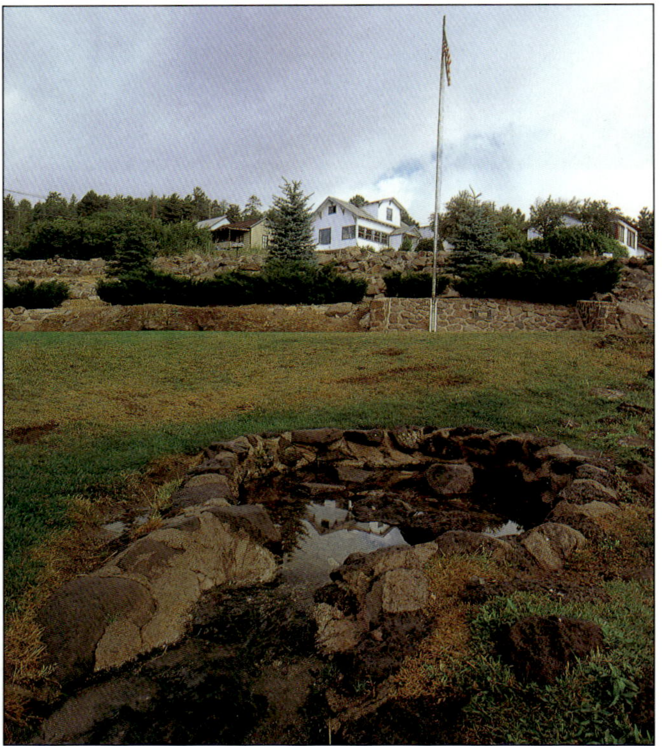

Flagstaff's colorful history has been well preserved in its downtown. (CLOCKWISE FROM ABOVE) *Flagstaff's original settlement clustered around Old Town Spring, west of today's downtown.* MICHAEL COLLIER
The restored Babbitt Building now features retail stores and offices. TOM BEAN
Part of the picturesque 1926 vintage train station serves as Flagstaff's busy visitor information center. OWEN F. LOWE

A couple of weeks after the railroad's arrival, a steam-powered sawmill began operations in what was called Mill Town. Chicago businessman Edward Ayer moved in to fulfill the railroad's demand for thousands of wooden ties. The blast of the mill whistle — morning, noon, and night — and the high-pitched whine of the saws meant jobs for more than 250 men, and a $200,000-a-year payroll.

Wood for the sawmill wasn't hard to find. Flagstaff was (and is) surrounded by the world's largest ponderosa pine forest. To reach the timber, mile after mile of spur rail line laced the hinterlands. From the 1880s into the 1940s, says historian Pat Stein, those lines "exploded" across the countryside, often laid out by little more than "taking a shot in the bush."

A tree was cut by two men pulling on either end of a crosscut saw, which they called a briar. A felled tree

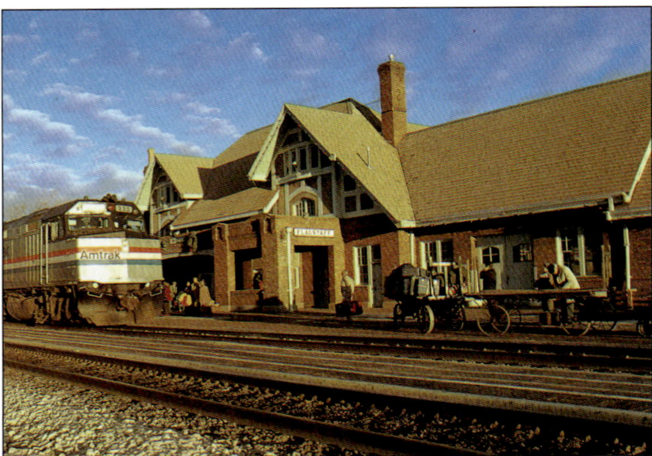

was bucked into logs, which were loaded on contraptions called big wheels, a pair of 12-foot-diameter spoked wheels. (You can see a pair at the Arizona Historical Society Pioneer Museum.) The logs were then pulled to the railhead by a team of draft horses and loaded onto flatcars.

A man toiling in the northern Arizona woods easily burned 7,000 calories in a 10-hour workday. Good food, and plenty of it, was necessary to keep loggers in a camp. At mealtimes, the lumberjacks sat down at long tables in the mess hall and wolfed down grub, observing the custom of silence at the table, save for a request to "shoot the beans." In logger lingo, coffee was referred to by its brand name, Arbuckle; pancakes were "blankets;" biscuits were "doorknobs." The cook, or "pot walloper," was a most important person in any logging camp. One who baked bread poorly soon earned the derogatory title of "sourdough cook."

The livestock industry in northern Arizona is older than the railroad — and just as important to the development and character of Flagstaff.

Sheep ranching began circa 1876 when Tennessean

Thomas McMillan arrived with a herd of woollies and settled in Flagstaff. McMillan, considered Flagstaff's first permanent white settler, built his home across from where the Museum of Northern Arizona now stands. The old McMillan place now houses the offices of the Grand Canyon Trust, a conservation organization. Other big sheep raisers in the region were C.H. Schulz, the Daggs brothers, Walter Hill, operating out by Government Springs, and Frank Hart, for whom Hart Prairie is named. Sheep were big business, and by 1887 more than 200,000 grazed across northern Arizona, producing two million pounds of fleece a season. Sheep generally cost four dollars, and a fleece went for one dollar.

Many sheepherders in Hart Prairie and around the Peaks were of Spanish and Basque heritage. During the long periods in camp, they often expressed their loneliness and pride in their homelands by carving on the white-barked aspen trees. The bold black letters on one large tree spell "Antonio Vasquez, 52 years, Badajoz, Spain."

In 1877, cattle ranching began. The Mormons settled at Leroux Spring, headquartering one of the first cattle companies there. They built a stockade of pine logs, calling it Fort Moroni. The area later became known as Fort Valley.

Brothers David and William Babbitt got off the train in Flagstaff in 1886, and immediately bought land and some cattle to which they applied their brand — CO Bar — for their home of Cincinnati, Ohio. Their three other brothers, George, Charles, and Edward, soon joined them, and the five Babbitts expanded their livestock operations and launched the Babbitt Brothers Trading Company, engaging in everything from selling dry goods to undertaking. The Babbitts' original 1888 sandstone building at the corner of Aspen and North San Francisco has been restored along with many others in a revitalized downtown Flagstaff. (A stroll with Dick and Sherry Mangum's "Flagstaff Historic Walk" booklet, available at many downtown shops, tells the stories behind the early structures.)

In 1904, a greenhorn by the name of Earle Forrest came to Flagstaff to cowboy for the Babbitts. He was a literate young man who was proud to work alongside the legendary cowboys of the CO Bar. Cowboys everywhere ate a lot of beef and the CO Bar hands were no exception. Forrest recalled that during his first days at the Cedar Ranch, part of the CO Bar, Eli Lucero showed him how Mexican cowboys cooked a delicacy — the head of a yearling. The head was rolled in a

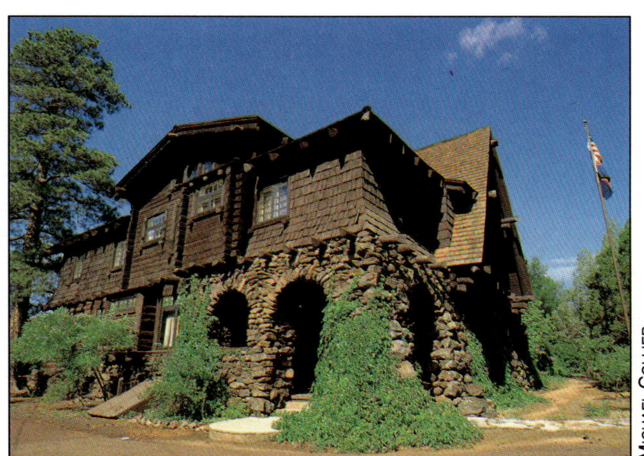

MICHAEL COLLIER

RIORDAN MANSION

In the summer of 1887, Denis Matthew Riordan bought the Ayer Lumber Company and delegated the job of running it to his younger brothers, Timothy and Michael.

In 1904, Timothy and Michael built a 13,000-square-foot mansion within sight of their mill. Charles Whittlesey, architect of the Grand Canyon's El Tovar Hotel, designed the mansion in the American Craftsman style popular at the turn of the century. The house was constructed of native wood and stone.

A porch and common living area, called the Rendezvous Room, joined the two wings of the Riordan house. Timothy and his family lived in one wing; Michael and his family in the other. The brothers married sisters, Caroline and Elizabeth Metz.

Now part of the Arizona State Park system, the Riordan Mansion is open for regular guided tours. On Timothy's side of the house, visitors can see the fine Tiffany stained glass windows, the 1884 billiard table, and the gorgeous 1904 Steinway piano. Beside the big stone fireplace in the living room reposes a pair of oversized shoes, which Tim called Paul Bunyan's baby shoes — good conversation starters.

Laughter ceased and dark silence engulfed the Riordan Mansion with the tragic death of Tim and Caroline's daughter Anna in 1927. She became ill the night of her engagement party and, two days later, died of polio. Standing in Anna's bedroom today, surrounded by her photographs and silk dresses, a person can palpably feel the poignancy of her death.

Riordan State Historic Park, 1300 Riordan Ranch Street, is open daily. For information on guided tours, call (602) 779-4395.

piece of hide, wrapped in a burlap sack, and buried in the dirt. A big fire was built over it, and the coals lasted all night. In the morning Eli dug out the head, removed the sack and hide, and the feast was ready. "Well it was good," Forrest declared, " meat, brains and tongue all well cooked . . . and we enjoyed it in spite of those big calf eyes staring at us."

The CO Bar (still owned by the Babbitt family) and a number of other ranches continue to graze cattle in the forests and on the rolling plains that surround Flagstaff.

In 1894, Bostonian Percival Lowell sent Andrew Ellicott Douglass to the West to locate the best site for an astronomical observatory. Lowell wanted to be ready for an upcoming close encounter between Earth and the planet Mars. After considering 10 other locations, Douglass informed Lowell that the high altitude and usually cloudless skies in the north part of the territory would provide the best viewing. (A.E. Douglass, incidentally, used the trees around Flagstaff in founding the science of dendrochronology, or tree-ring dating.)

The observatory's telescopes were located atop what soon became known as Mars Hill, overlooking the freshly incorporated town of Flagstaff, already calling itself the Skylight City.

Percival Lowell arrived in late May of 1894 to establish the observatory and begin his viewing of the red planet. He asserted that he saw "canals" on Mars — a sure sign of some form of intelligent life — a theory, one that stirred lively scientific debate and public interest.

Lowell also calculated the existence of a ninth planet, beyond Neptune, in our solar system. On February 18, 1930, Kansas farm boy and fledgling astronomer Clyde Tombaugh discovered the planet Pluto from photographs taken on the 13-inch telescope on Mars Hill.

V.M. Slipher, director of Lowell Observatory at the time of the Pluto discovery, also made significant findings. Slipher presented evidence that galaxies called spiral nebulae are receding from Earth at speeds of up to two million miles an hour, leading to the now-accepted idea that the universe is expanding.

Today, Lowell is still very much a working observatory with a staff of more than a dozen astronomers and technicians studying the heavens. Ted Bowell, one of

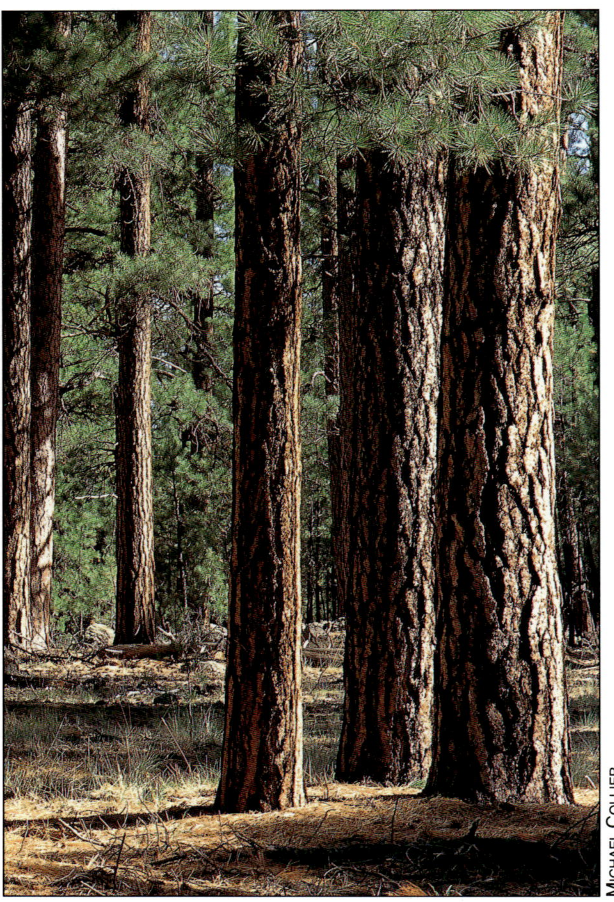

Michael Collier

G.A. Pearson Natural Area

From the earliest days, Flagstaff has been a center for forestry. In 1909, the Forest Service sent Gustaf Adolph Pearson to Flagstaff to start its first research facility. For 30 years Gus Pearson conducted studies on ponderosa pines at the Fort Valley Experimental Station. Today, 60 acres have been set aside as the G.A. Pearson Natural Area. There you can see what the forests of the Southwest looked like before the lumber industry arrived. Magnificent old-growth "yellow pines," ponderosas that have lived 200 and 300 years, stand undisturbed.

Members of the forestry school at Northern Arizona University still use the Pearson area for their research. Chuck Avery is one who has kept track of the same trees that Gus Pearson did. Pausing at a fallen ponderosa in a sunlit spot, Avery said he's learned that it takes a mighty ponderosa pine nearly as long to die as it did to live. Though they are no longer producing green needles, dead ponderosas, whether standing or fallen, are vital homes for cavity-nesting birds, insects, and other wildlife in the forest.

The Pearson area is located eight miles northwest of Flagstaff on U.S. Route 180. Turn left (west) onto Forest Road 222, just past mile marker 224.

those astronomers, is a preeminent asteroid finder with more than 300 to his credit. Part of the privilege of discovering asteroids is naming them. He and Lowell colleague Brian Skiff discovered four asteroids in 1983 and 1984 and named them Lennon, McCartney, Harrison, and Starr, for, you guessed it, the Beatles.

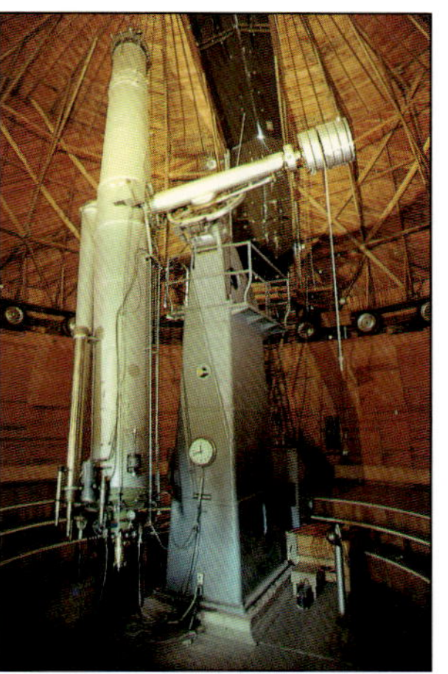

Lowell Observatory maintains an active public program with regularly scheduled lectures and viewings. Just in time for the observatory's centennial in 1994, the new Steele Visitor Center opened on Mars Hill featuring interactive exhibits, a simulated observatory, and a lecture hall.

Several nights each week, the historic 24-inch Clark telescope Lowell used is open for public viewing. The "Clark," as it's affectionately known, is a refractor telescope purchased from famed Alvan Clark & Sons of Cambridge, Massachusetts. When the telescope is available, shivering visitors brave the evening chill to line up at the dome for a chance to look through the eyepiece at the moon, Jupiter, or other celestial objects, which appear exceptionally sharp in the usually dry, transparent air of northern Arizona. The original dome, 8,000 pounds and built of ponderosa pine planks, creaks and groans as it rotates on its ring of 1954 Ford pickup truck wheels and tires. The opening in the dome must align with the 30-ton telescope to allow it to track its selected point in the sky.

Another telescope, the one used in Pluto's discovery, can be seen on the grounds at Lowell Observatory as well. (For information on programs and tour times at Lowell, call 602-774-2096.)

Several other astronomical centers make Flagstaff their home. Northern Arizona University's observatory on campus features a 24-inch reflecting telescope that is open for viewing on Friday nights, weather permitting. And a branch of the U.S. Naval Observatory is located four miles west of town, housing the Navy's largest optical telescope. (Tours must be specially arranged.)

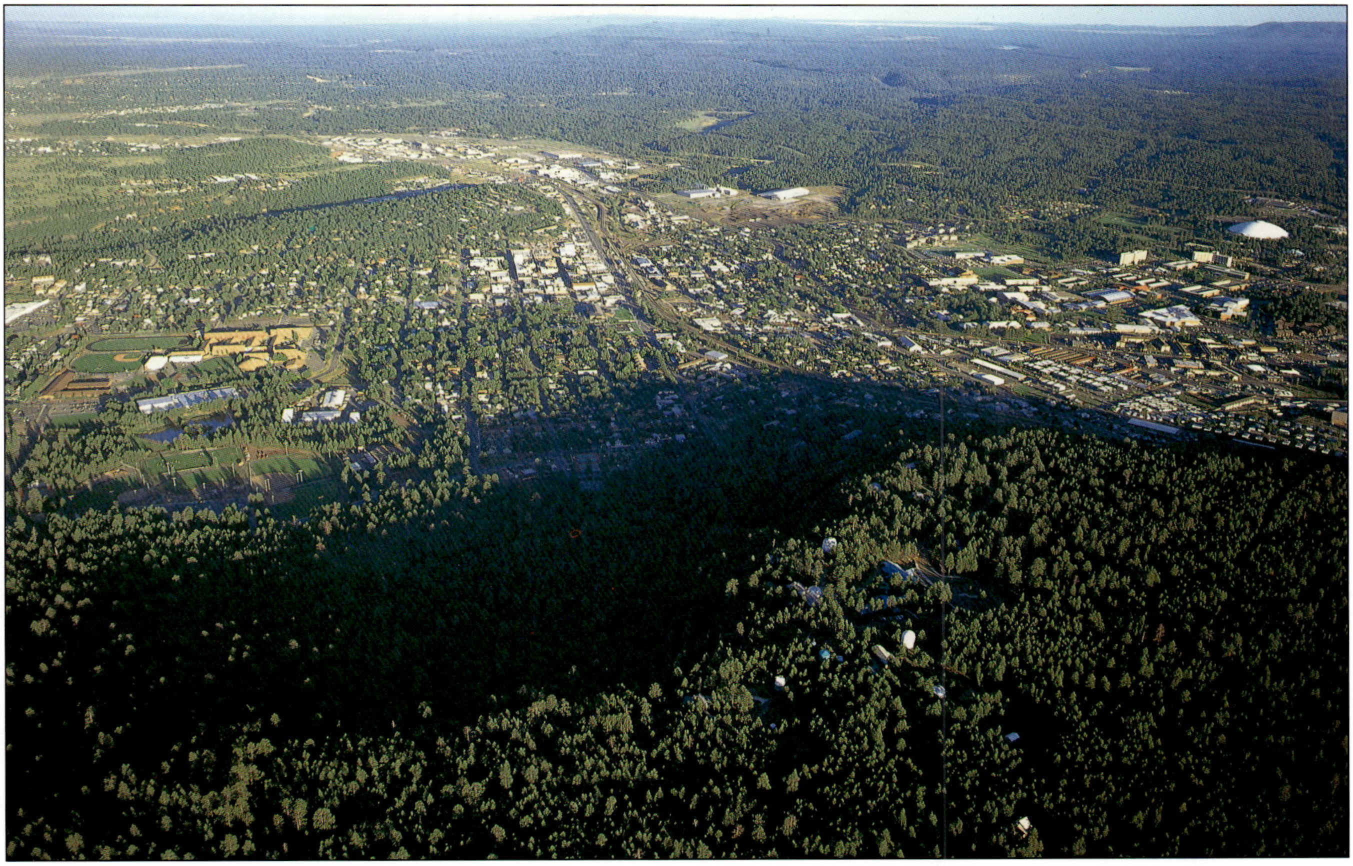

(TOP) *The Clark telescope used by Percival Lowell in his observations of Mars dominates the interior of Lowell Observatory's ponderosa pine dome.* FRANK ZULLO (ABOVE) *An aerial view shows the Lowell Observatory on Mars Hill and downtown Flagstaff beyond.* MICHAEL COLLIER

Graduation is anything but a solemn occasion at Northern Arizona University. Close to 2,000 students in black robes and mortarboard caps fill the floor of the Skydome for spring commencement. They wave, whoop, and cheer to friends and family in the packed stands as their names are called — Martin, Manygoats, Ortega, Houlihan, Ramirez, Baker, Nielsen, Murphy, O'Reilly, Pelligrini, Gee, Wu, Salleh, Yaacob, Yazzie. And the supporters in the stands cheer back in celebration of those who have earned degrees in business, education, psychology, biology, and other fields.

Northern Arizona University (NAU) is the state's third–largest university with an enrollment approaching 16,000 students. Along with a strong focus on undergraduate education, NAU's specialties include schools of forestry and hotel and restaurant management, a master's level physical therapy program, and Native American studies.

Throughout the year, NAU's Ardrey Auditorium is the location of musical and theatrical performances by students and faculty. Next to Ardrey is the university's Cline Library, more than doubled in size after a major addition in 1992. Its shelves now hold more than a million volumes.

NAU is home to a rare type of pottery kiln, the only one of its kind in the Western Hemisphere. In 1984 NAU ceramics professor Don Bendel met master Japanese potter Yukio Yamamoto. A year later, Yamamoto, with the help of many people in Flagstaff, built a five-chambered, wood-burning *noborigama tozan* kiln. "Noborigama" means "climbing kiln," and "tozan" means "east mountain," where these original ancient kilns were built.

NAU students have plenty of opportunities to engage in athletics. Men's and women's teams, the Lumberjacks and Lady Jacks, compete in the Big Sky Conference. The swimming and diving teams, which belong to the Pacific Coast Swim Conference, have won several conference championships in recent years. The state-of-the-art indoor natatorium is a favored high-altitude training site for swimmers from all over the world.

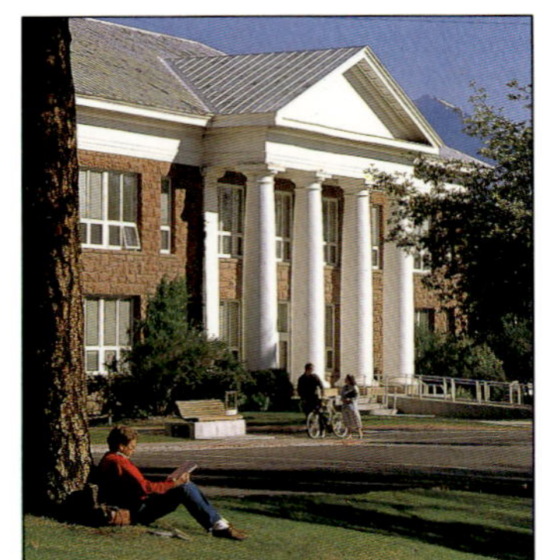

The NAU practice fields near the Skydome are the high-altitude summer training site for the Arizona Cardinals football team. Mid-morning and mid-afternoon practices are open to the public.

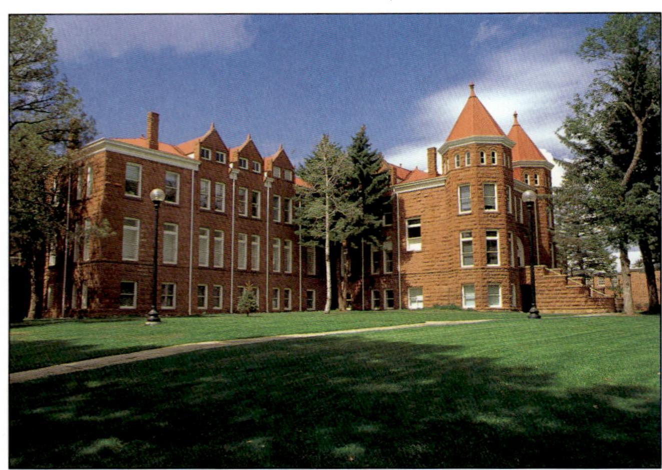

(CLOCKWISE FROM TOP) *White columned facades, ivy covered walls, and tall pines give Northern Arizona University an Ivy League appearance.* DON B. STEVENSON
Venerable Old Main, the school's first building, has served a variety of uses in its first century — from classrooms to dormitory to today's incarnation as an art gallery. MICHAEL COLLIER
School is back in session on the tidy NAU campus as autumn leaves change on the San Francisco Peaks. PETER BLOOMER

The first building on campus was Old Main, built in 1894 to house the reform school that six years later became the Arizona Normal School. Located at Knoles Drive and McMullen Circle at the entrance to NAU's historic north campus, the twin-turreted, recently renovated red sandstone building now houses NAU's Art Museum and Galleries, featuring rotating exhibits and the Marguerite Hettel Weiss Art Museum. Open Monday through Friday 8 a.m. to 5 p.m., and Sundays 1 p.m. to 4 p.m. Admission is free and patron parking is available in front. Phone (602) 523-3471 for information on current exhibits.

One of northern Arizona's big attractions is the four-season climate. Spring can come late and often seems too short. Some say were it not for the notorious winds and snow on the tulips, spring might be missed altogether.

But summers are what everyone waits for and by Memorial Day, the splendid season is in full swing. June shines sunny and warm with cool crisp nights. Locals don't want to leave, and desert dwellers flock to this cool, green haven of the north.

It's perfect weather for a bike ride and I decide to try out the new Flagstaff Urban Trails System, better known as "FUTS." This partially completed network of unpaved trails is designed for nonmotorized uses — people can bicycle, walk, jog, and cross-country ski along it. The trails eventually will connect parks, neighborhoods, schools, shopping, and work places throughout Flagstaff as well as intersect with trails on adjoining federal and state lands. FUTS is a great way for visitors to get acquainted with Flagstaff.

I stopped by city hall and asked planner Mike Conner for a map of the trail system and took off. Starting my ride at Fort Tuthill County Park south of town, the path took me past shopping centers, across the campus of Northern Arizona University, and into downtown. From there I pieced my way on side streets through West Flagstaff and, back on FUTS, rode past the duck pond, Thorpe Park, north along the Rio de Flag, where willows were in bud and crab apple trees in blush pink bloom, to where the trail ends at Crescent Street.

A secondary leg of the trail system now leads to Buffalo Park, on McMillan Mesa between the east and west sides of town. Named for a herd of bison released there in the 1960s, Buffalo Park is an open prairie with spectacular views of the San Francisco Peaks. The buffalo eventually were moved to another preserve because they kept ending up in people's yards, but the park is still a popular area for joggers and bicyclists and serves as a departure point for trails onto Mount Elden, into the Dry Lake Hills, and up into the San Francisco Peaks. A map posted at the park entrance shows the routes.

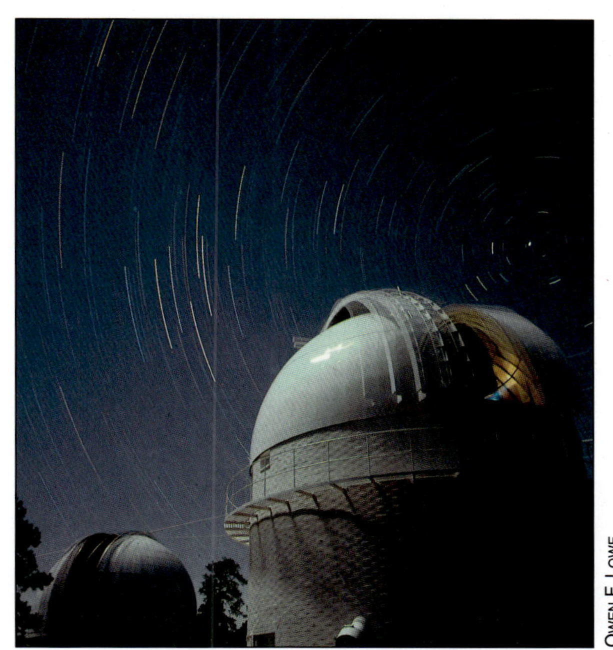

Owen F. Lowe

Flagstaff Festival of Science

Want to help excavate an archaeological site? Gaze at stars or planets through a telescope? Learn more about what killed off the dinosaurs? During Flagstaff's annual Festival of Science, you can do these things, and much more. Held in early autumn each year, the festival aims to make science interesting and accessible to the public — children and adults alike.

A number of Flagstaff institutions, businesses, and disciplines, including astronomical observatories, the Arboretum, Museum of Northern Arizona, Northern Arizona University, the U.S. Geological Survey, the Forest Service, and W.L. Gore, manufacturer of medical devices and high-tech fibers and fabrics, open their doors to the public during the 10-day festival.

Well-known explorers, scientists, and authors serve as keynote speakers. Talks, tours, open houses, classroom visits, and field trips are on the festival's agenda as well.

Mid-July through September mornings dawn bright and clear, but by noontime cumulonimbus clouds are building cottony towers in the sky. By mid-afternoon they darken to blue-black and toss jagged lightning bolts from cloud to cloud and from cloud to the ground. Thunder booms and, just in time for an afternoon *siesta*, the cooling rains come. You can almost set your watch by them. In an hour or two the clouds break up and move off leaving the clean, fresh smell of the forest.

Summer in Flagstaff is festival time — rodeo, powwow, craft shows, and arts festivals, with new events scheduled each year.

A long-standing summer tradition in Flagstaff held the last weekend in July, the *Indian Days PowWow* draws participants from Nebraska, New Mexico, Arizona, and as far away as Saskatchewan, Canada. Indian men, women, boys, and girls dance to hypnotic drum beating. Older women perform more traditional, sedate dances; the younger girls fly out into the arena like butterflies "fancy dancing" in their feathers and fringe.

Violet and Steve Bird of Tuba City, Arizona, proudly show a photograph of their five-year-old granddaughter dressed in her outfit. (Outfit is the proper term, they stress, not costume: "costumes are for clowns.") Children start young, some as soon as they can walk. They learn by watching others and then come up with their own style. Powwows, the Birds explain, are social, not ceremonial, dances. Through their movements, the dancers tell stories. Men, for example, may reenact a hunting scene.

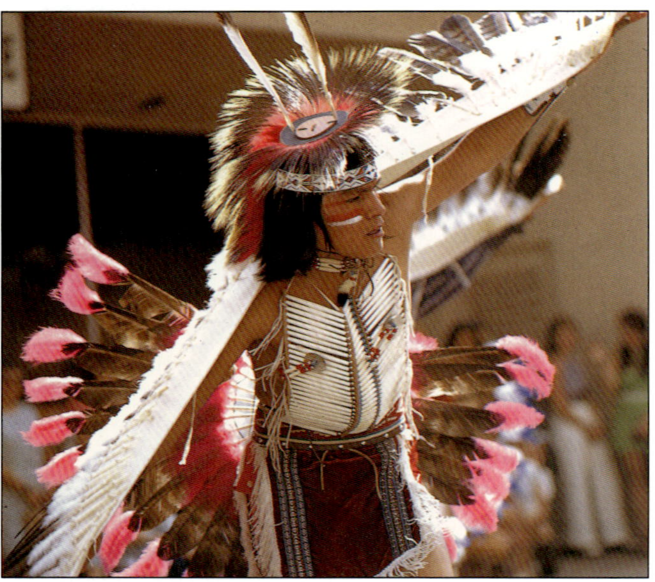

Dances start Saturday morning, last late into the night, and continue through Sunday. The Grand Entry features all the dancers in the arena in an eye-dazzling display of colors. Cash prizes go to the dancers for their rhythm, style, and outfits.

For nearly 30 summers, the *Flagstaff Festival of the Arts* has served up a feast of music, dance, theater, and other performing arts. The festival started in 1966, a few years after Dr. Pat Curry, former music director at Northern Arizona University, came up with the idea.

The festival's ambitious calendar is jammed from July into early August with guest artists, performances by the festival's fine orchestra, chamber music brunches, a Native American Cultural Weekend, poetry readings, art exhibits, dance, films, and live theater. Some of the events are held outdoors in the refreshing, cool air. Telephone (800) 266-7740 or (602) 774-7750 for schedule and admission information.

Throughout the rest of the year, there is an active arts schedule. The Flagstaff Symphony, in its fourth decade, performs each season. Theatrikos, the community theater, offers a full round of productions. For symphony schedule and tickets, contact 774-5107. For Theatrikos, call 774-1662.

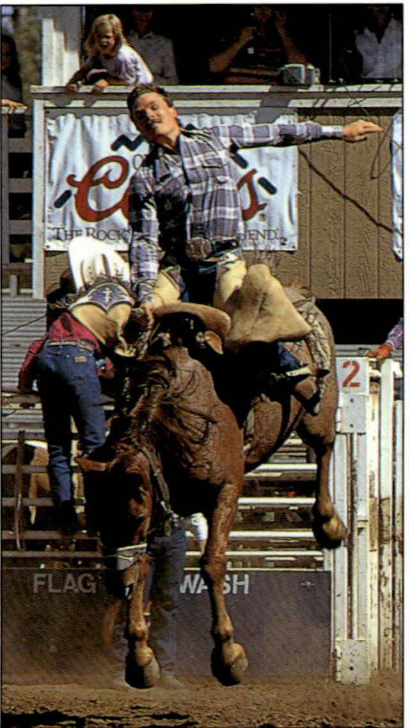

Spectators hanging on the fences . . . cowboys wearing pressed shirts, white straw hats, and blue jeans with the outline of Copenhagen cans embossed on the back pockets . . . rodeo queens fluttering about, their curls and gold shirts glittering. It's the *Pine Country Pro Rodeo*, held in mid-June at Fort Tuthill County Park, three miles southwest of downtown Flagstaff on State Route 89A. A street dance, parade, pancake breakfast, and festive happenings precede the rodeo. But the big event is the rodeo itself — bareback and saddle back bronc riding, barrel racing, calf and team roping, steer wrestling, and the grand finale, bull riding.

Want to see the biggest pumpkin grown in the county, a jar of golden wildflower honey, or a prize sheep? Then head on out to the *Coconino County Fair*, held Labor Day Weekend at Fort Tuthill County Park just south of Flagstaff on State Route 89A. There are stomach-churning carnival rides, corn on the cob and fry bread, and plenty of good family fun.

For more information on Flagstaff's festivals contact the Flagstaff Convention and Visitors Bureau, (602) 779-7611; or the Flagstaff Visitors Center, (800) 842-7293.

In late summer, sunflowers spangle roadsides and fields with gold, and rabbitbrush and purple asters bloom. Inevitably, on an afternoon in August an almost imperceptible change occurs in the light. "Did you feel fall in the air today?" I ask my husband. He agrees, but with hesitation. Neither of us wants to admit that summer is coming to an end. Admittedly, autumn is a golden time of warm, dry days and cool nights, when groves of aspens glow in the mountains, but with winter nipping at its heels, it always comes too soon. The tomatoes in the garden are barely ripe when it's time to cut and haul firewood again. And as the leaves begin to flutter from the aspen branches, we gather with friends and place bets in the Snow Pool. Everyone picks a date when he or she thinks enough snow will fall in town to make a snowball. It's on the honor system, but there's usually little doubt. (Losers all chip in and buy the victor dinner at a chosen restaurant.)

And then comes winter. Platt Cline, veteran of more than 50 of them in the northland, maintains that winter is the "sorting process" for people who think they might like to live here.

Truth be told, winters aren't all that bad. It does get cold, but most of the time it's sunny. When it does snow, two or three feet from one storm isn't too unusual. Snowfall each winter averages about 95 inches. That takes into consideration winters like 1972-73, when Flagstaff received a record 210 inches of snow, and 1933-34, when only 11 inches fell. Thanksgiving and Easter usually bracket the snow season, though that is by no means a hard and fast rule.

In years when the snow season appears to be a bust, locals have been known to build bonfires and do snow dances to bring on the fluffy stuff. The amount of winter snowfall is more than a matter of pure recreational interest; snowfall replenishes the springs on the Peaks, and meltwater fills reservoirs and underground water supplies that quench the town's thirst.

Inevitably the storms do come, and after they pass, the sun and the skiers come out. Compared to many upscale resort areas, the ski season in Flagstaff and neighboring Williams is a real bargain. Many motel rooms are modestly priced, and lift tickets for the Arizona Snowbowl and the Williams downhill ski area are still affordable for most people. Opportunities also abound for cross-country skiing on miles of forest roads and along groomed trails at Nordic centers where instruction and rental equipment are available.

Care to ice skate? Drop by the Jay Lively Activity Center in McPherson Park at 1850 North Turquoise Drive. It's open to the public for indoor ice skating during the winter months.

Each year, in the middle of February, *Flagstaff Winterfest* celebrates the season with every conceivable kind of winter and snow-related activity scheduled: llama games, snowball softball, telemark clinics, stargazing, storytelling, food fests, dances, concerts, and dogsled races.

Cheryl Crum, a musher in the two-day dogsled races, confesses she's been "wacko" over dogsledding since the day someone gave her a husky. Now she spends her days training and taking care of nearly 30 sled dogs at her home outside Flagstaff. Lined up in the chute at the Winterfest race, four of her dogs strain at the ropes tied to her sled, anchored in the snow with a mean-looking steel hook. Cheryl stands alert, with both feet hard on the brake. She knows her dogs can rocket out of the chute at 20 miles an hour, and holding them back until officials start the race is a challenge.

With the report of the starting gun and a cacophony of yelps and barks they were off racing across the snow-covered meadows and forests around Flagstaff. Cheryl's hours of training paid off. She and her dogs placed second.

Winter, spring, summer, and fall, Flagstaff has something to offer during every season, and for every interest — a sense of history, friendly people, infectious vitality, and beautiful surroundings.

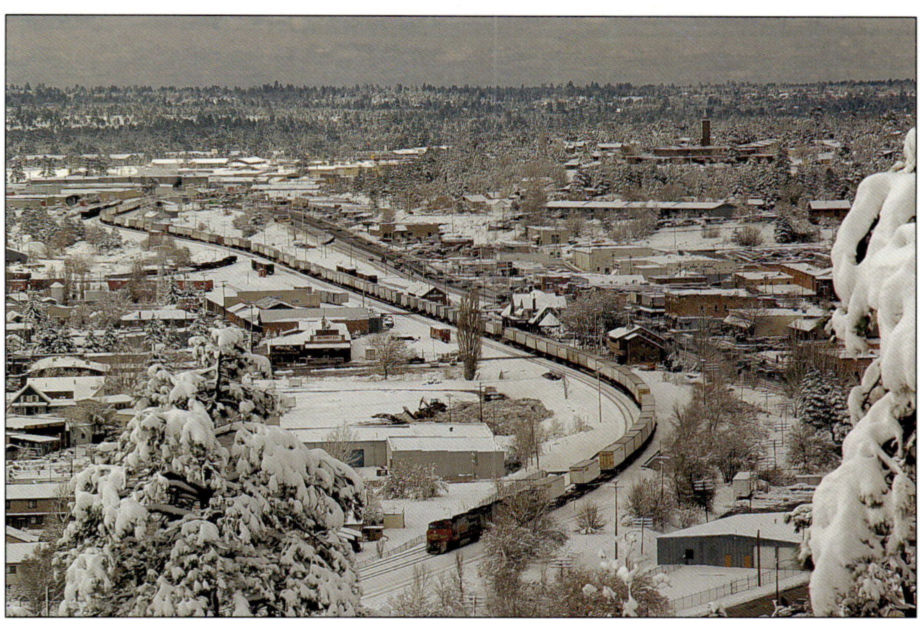

(OPPOSITE PAGE) *Flagstaff's Indian Days Pow Wow and the Pine Country Rodeo attract Indian dancers and rodeo cowboys from all over North America.*
PETER BLOOMER AND MICHAEL COLLIER
(ABOVE) *A train rumbles through a wintry downtown Flagstaff.*
DAMON BULLOCK

Places To Go

Museum of Northern Arizona — One of Flagstaff's most venerable institutions, the Museum of Northern Arizona was founded in 1928 by Dr. Harold Colton, a marine biologist turned archaeologist, and his wife, Mary-Russell Ferrell Colton. Dr. Colton was attracted to northern Arizona in the early 1900s from Philadelphia. He and Mary-Russell

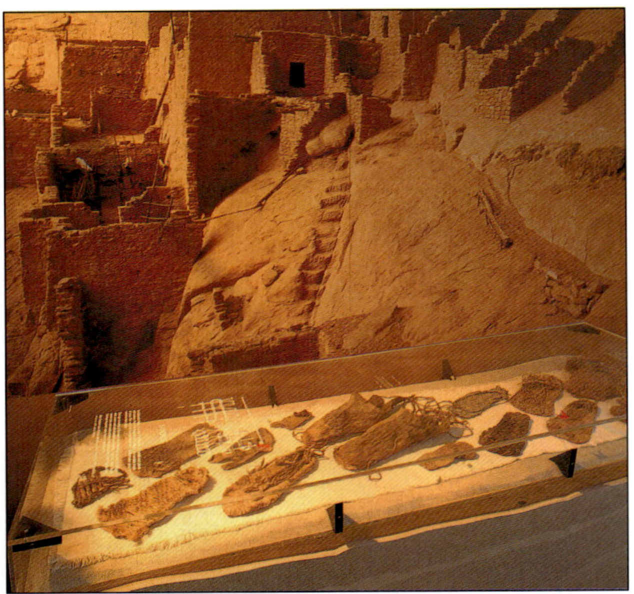

honeymooned on the San Francisco Peaks, and thereafter spent several summers in Flagstaff. They liked it so much they decided to relocate and spend the rest of their lives exploring the cultural and natural wonders of northern Arizona.

The Coltons' interest in Native American arts and crafts led to the museum's first Hopi Artists Exhibition (held annually for more than 60 years), along with the later Navajo and Zuni shows. The three are now the museum's biggest events. From June through August, thousands of people come to peruse and purchase traditional and contemporary rugs, pottery, basketry, jewelry, sculpture, paintings, and other works.

MNA, as it's known, also features permanent exhibits in anthropology, geology, biology, and fine arts, along with a number of changing exhibits with emphasis on the Colorado Plateau.

While you're visiting, take time to stroll the Rio de Flag Nature Trail which heads down into the basalt-walled canyon in front of the museum. In a half-mile, you'll see grapevines, horsetails, willows, irises, and monkeyflowers — plants that take advantage of the ephemeral water.

MNA, three miles northwest of downtown on Fort Valley Road (U.S. Route 180), is open every day, 9 a.m. to 5 p.m., except Thanksgiving, Christmas, and New Year's. Contact the Museum of Northern Arizona, Route 4, Box 720, Flagstaff, AZ 86001, (602) 774-5213. There is an admission charge for nonmembers.

Arizona Historical Society Pioneer Museum — In the early days of this century, the Pioneer Museum was the county hospital for the indigent. Patients were not always happy to be at the "poor farm." One cowboy, in for a broken leg, found the hospital's battleship-gray walls so depressing that he offered his doctor any sum of money to move him to a hotel in town.

Now, the two-story, turn-of-the-century stone building on the north side of Fort Valley Road is a more cheerful place. If you're lucky, director Joe Meehan will come out, his handlebar mustache waxed to a golden shine, and regale you with stories

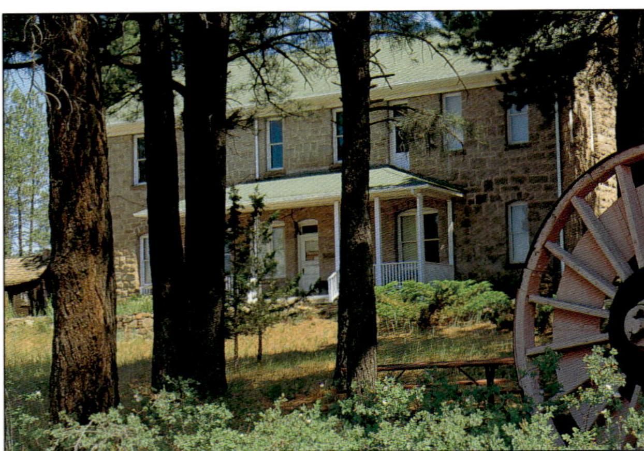

(ABOVE, LEFT) *An exhibit of woven sandals at the Museum of Northern Arizona helps visitors interpret the region's prehistory.* KERRICK JAMES

(ABOVE) *The Historical Society Pioneer Museum presents artifacts such as the 12-foot diameter "big wheels" once used by loggers.* JOHN DREW

of early-day Flagstaff. If Joe isn't there, you can still see memorabilia and exhibits of those days — fire-fighting equipment, old toys and games, medical items, and ranching and logging tools.

The museum's big annual celebration is the Independence Day Festival at which costumed interpreters demonstrate pioneer arts, crafts, and skills.

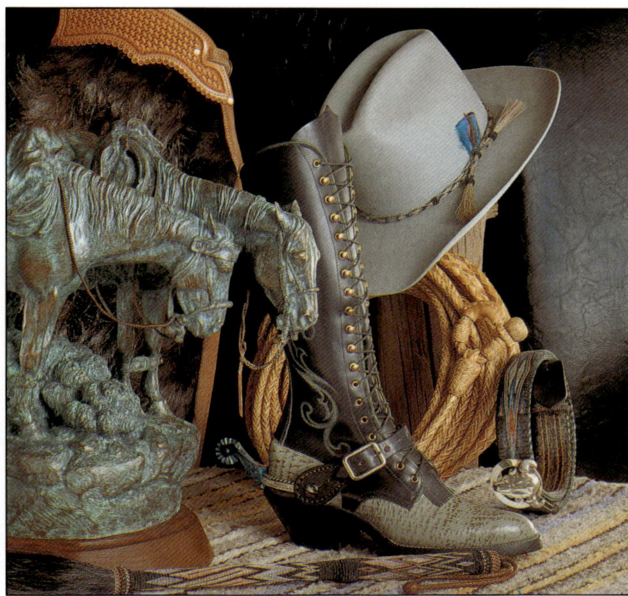

Open 9 a.m. to 5 p.m. Monday through Saturday; closed Sundays, Christmas, New Year's, Easter, and Thanksgiving. No admission charge, donations requested. Located across from the Museum of Northern Arizona, three miles northwest of downtown on Fort Valley Road (U.S. Route 180). Phone 774-6272.

Coconino Center for the Arts — Just behind the Pioneer Museum stands a glass-front, modern building dedicated to performances and art exhibits. Care for a set of hand-tooled silver spurs for just $8,900? Drop in at the Trappings of the American West show, which opens at the Coconino Center for the Arts each May. "Trappings" features some of the finest contemporary silverwork, leatherwork, and other arts and crafts of working cowboys and cowgirls in the West, along with films, workshops, cowboy poetry, and a dance and barbecue.

Throughout the year at the Coconino Center, you can see art exhibits, musical performances, and, from late June to early August, the Festival of Native American Arts. Call (602) 779-6921 for current information.

The Arboretum at Flagstaff — Officially the Transition Zone Horticultural Institute, this facility is called by most everybody simply "The Arboretum." This is the highest-elevation arboretum in the country, and demonstration gardens feature drought-resistant plants suited to the highlands of the Colorado Plateau. Visitors can view displays in the visitor center, stroll the peaceful paths through the gardens, or join guided tours. The Arboretum is open year-round. There is an admission charge for nonmembers. It is located 3.8 miles south on Woody Mountain Road off Route 66 just west of Flagstaff. Call (602) 774-1441 for visiting hours and tour times.

Other Attractions — For current information on things to do and places to go in Flagstaff, contact:

Flagstaff Chamber of Commerce at (800) 842-7293 or the Flagstaff Convention and Visitors Bureau at (602) 779-7611. Or, drop by the city's visitor center in the restored Amtrak station on Route 66 in historic downtown Flagstaff.

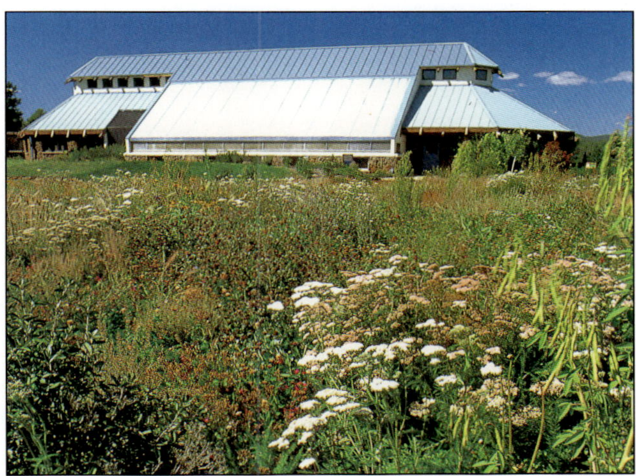

(ABOVE, LEFT) *Fine cowboy arts are among the varied regional works that yearly grace the Coconino Center for the Arts.* PETER BLOOMER (ABOVE) *The Arboretum at Flagstaff features an impressive collection of high elevation arid-lands plants.* STEWART AITCHISON

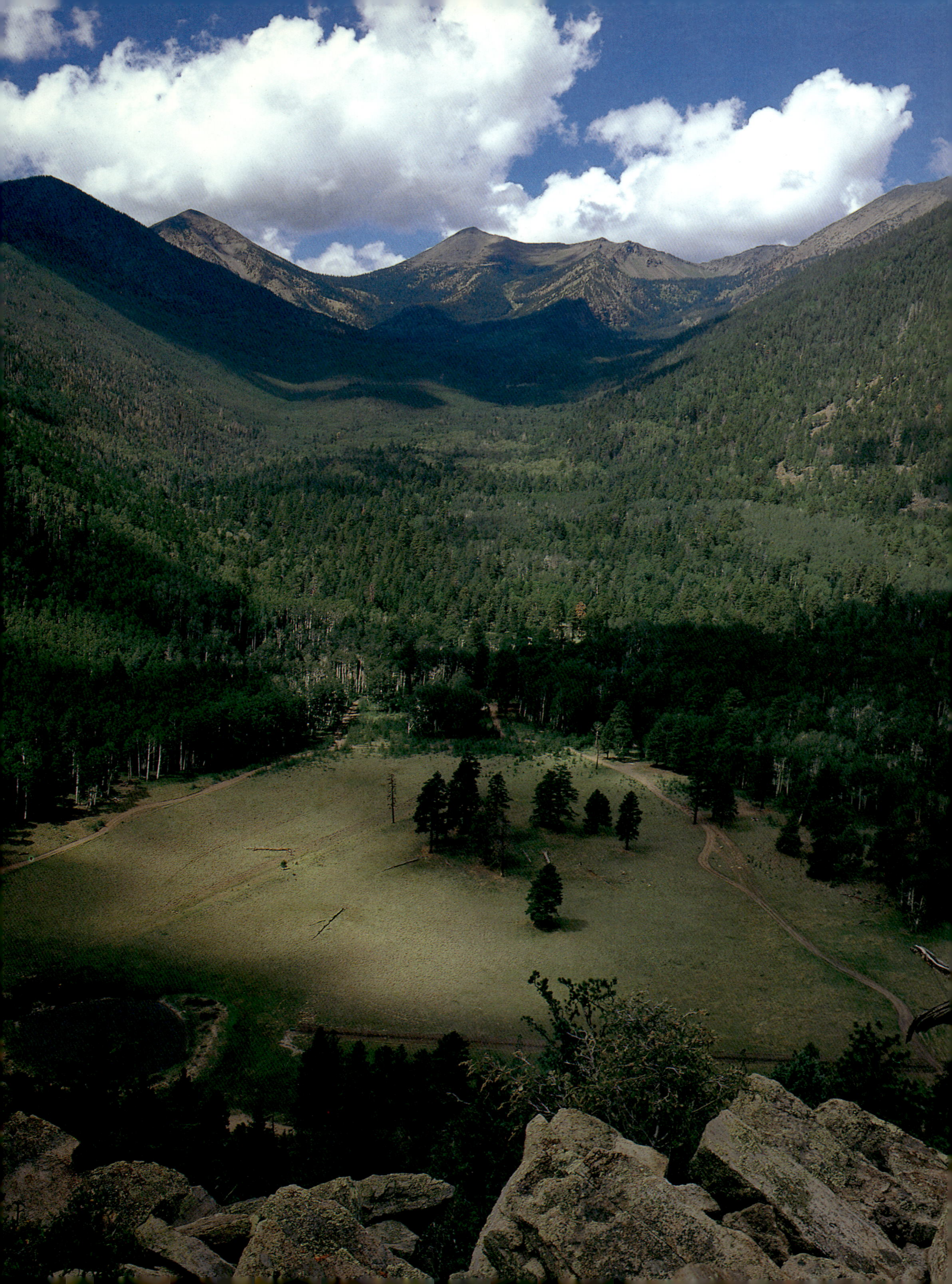

Chapter Two

The San Francisco Peaks

Exploring the Sacred Mountains

From throughout northern Arizona, you can see the elegant profile of the San Francisco Peaks. From whatever direction when I'm coming home, as soon as I glimpse their silhouettes I feel safe, anchored, drawn.

At first, the mountains' height, mass, and profile overpower. But a closer view completely alters those initial perceptions. I got that closer view on my 30th birthday when some friends and I hiked up Mount Humphreys, the summit of the Peaks.

We walked through dark forests of corkbark fir, Engelmann spruce, and aspen, their pale trunks bowed by the weight of previous winters' snows. Yellow columbines smiled beside the trail.

Not far beyond, we passed the tree line into tundra. Tiny alpine plants hugged the ground, and gnarled bristlecone pines endured on the scree slopes. At the saddle between Agassiz and Humphreys, we stared down into the greensward of the Inner Basin. The trail continued across lichen-splotched rock to what appeared to be our final destination.

Soon I learned the meaning of "false summit," for when we reached what surely had to be the top, it wasn't. My lungs had started burning at the 10,000-foot mark. The air had gotten noticeably thinner.

One last push, and we reached the top — 12,643 feet above sea level, the highest point in Arizona. From there it felt like we should be able to see the ocean. Instead, we gazed upon a sea of land that takes in the Grand Canyon, Echo Cliffs, Kendrick, Sitgreaves, and Mormon mountains, Hopi and Navajo Indian lands, and the blue dome of Navajo Mountain straddling the Arizona-Utah border. Surely this must be the center of the universe. At least, the center of my universe.

The San Francisco Peaks hold different meanings for different people. Other hikers, like my father-in-law, Bill Collier, and his friend, Ed Clapp, with whom I hiked to the top of Humphreys 10 years after my first trip, tried them on for size. They were getting ready for their annual hike in the Sierra Nevada and considered the Peaks a good warmup excursion.

Each winter, Flagstaffian George Bain and his family

(OPPOSITE PAGE) *The inspiring view of the San Francisco Peaks and the Inner Basin from Lockett Meadow is one of the finest sights in Arizona.* RICHARD WESTON
(FOLLOWING PANEL, PAGES 26 AND 27) *Glistening snow often caps the San Francisco Peaks in autumn.* RANDY PRENTICE

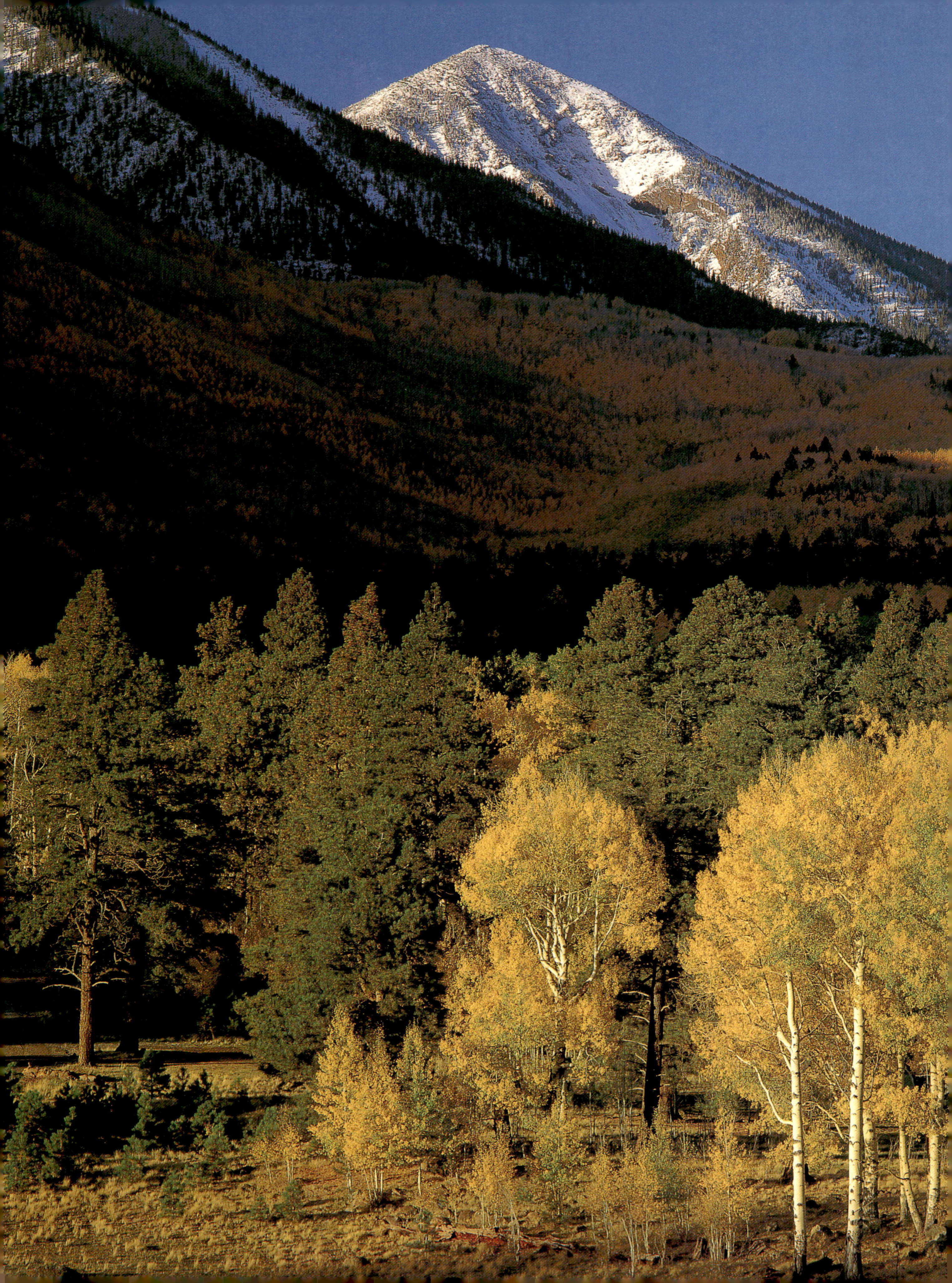

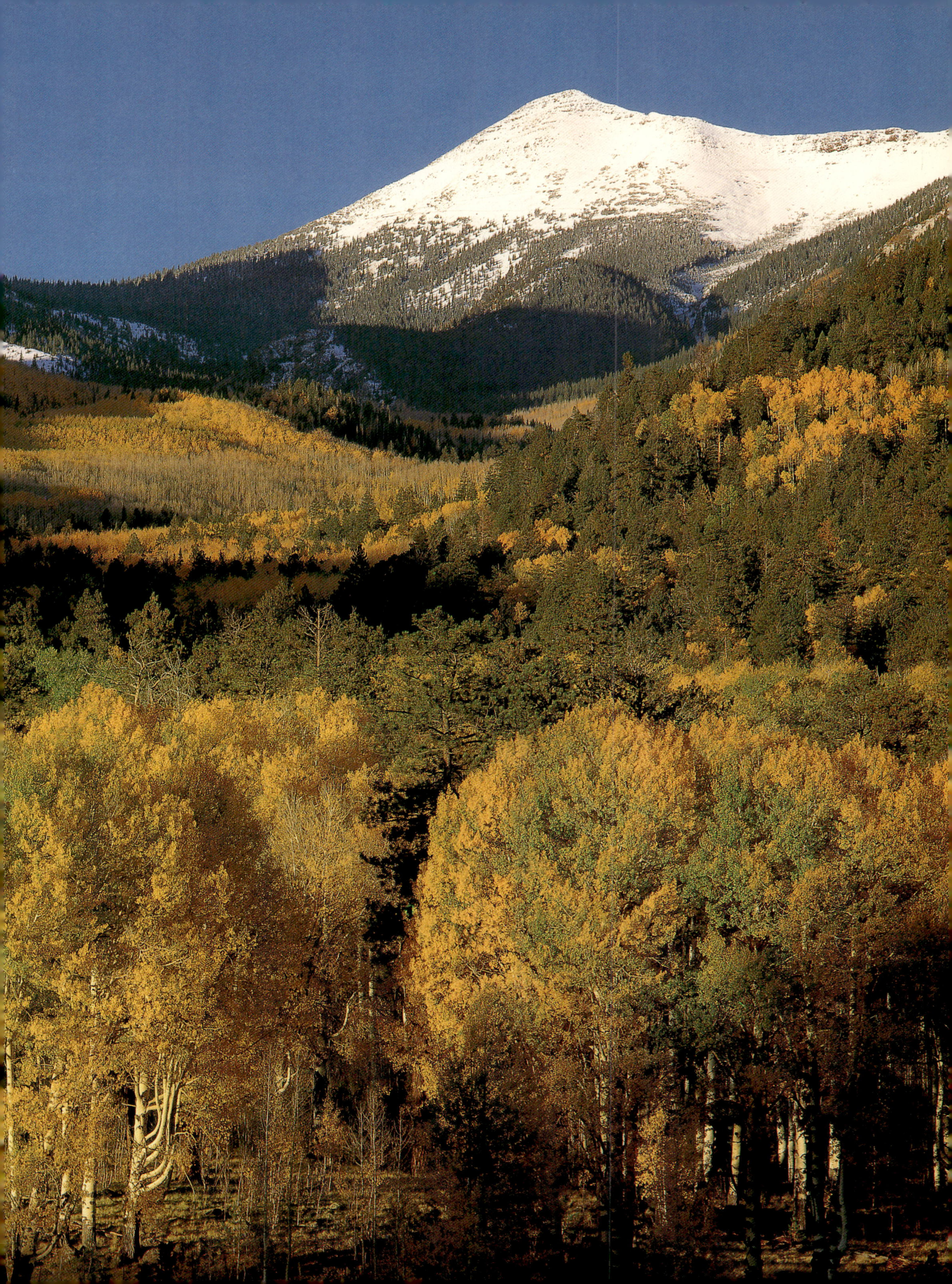

head for the steepest runs down Agassiz, hooked on the thrill of fast downhill skiing. My husband recalls a winter cross-country ski expedition when he and his *compadres* spent two nights in tents on the Peaks, the wind howling through the saddle at 60 miles an hour.

Forest Service botanist Barb Phillips searches the Peaks for rare floral wonders, like the San Francisco Peaks groundsel that grows nowhere else in the world. Astronomers have lugged telescopes up the Peaks, hoping to get a better view of the heavens.

Neighboring Native Americans hold these mountains in special regard. The Hopi call the Peaks *Nuvatukya'ovi*, "Snowy Mountain High Place." They are the summer home of the *katsinam* or kachinas, spirits to whom they pray for rain. The top of Agassiz Peak, the one they call Spring Flower, is now off lim-

Around the Peaks Loop Drive

Gas up and clean the windshield before you leave town. This 60-mile journey offers a scenic, back-road circumnavigation of the San Francisco Peaks. About half the trip is on dirt or gravel roads, all passable with a normal passenger vehicle almost anytime from May through October.

Head north from downtown Flagstaff on Highway 89. Just past the turnoff to Sunset Crater, turn left onto Forest Road 418. The road climbs through an open forest of ponderosa pine, past shallow, rocky canyons, with Mount Humphreys, the highest of the Peaks, on your left side.

There are plenty of opportunities to get out and stretch your legs. About seven miles in you'll see a sign for Forest Road 9123J, leading to the Aubineau and Bear Jaw trails. The road into the trailhead passes a pair of livestock ponds called Reese Tanks. It's tempting to linger here, but there's more to see.

Back on 418, you'll pass the White Horse Hills and groves of white-trunked aspen, many bearing the carvings of early sheepherders and claw marks of black bears. At the junction with Forest Road 151, you can turn left for a tour south through Hart Prairie, a beautiful drive especially in the fall when the aspens are turning. But be warned it also is a very popular, heavily traveled, narrow road. It ends at U.S. 180, and a left turn will take you back toward town.

If the roads are fairly dry, you might prefer taking a look at another interesting natural feature, Lava River Cave. To get there take a right turn at the junction with Forest Road 151. In a mile and a half you'll reach U.S. 180. Turn left (south) and drive 5.5 miles. Turn right on Forest Road 245. If the roads are wet you'll need four-wheel drive to go farther. Drive three miles and turn left on FR171 for a mile. Turn left again on FR 171B which will take you to the fenced parking area. A path leads to the entrance to Lava River Cave.

In 1915, loggers discovered this gaping opening in the forest floor leading to a 4,000-foot-long sub-

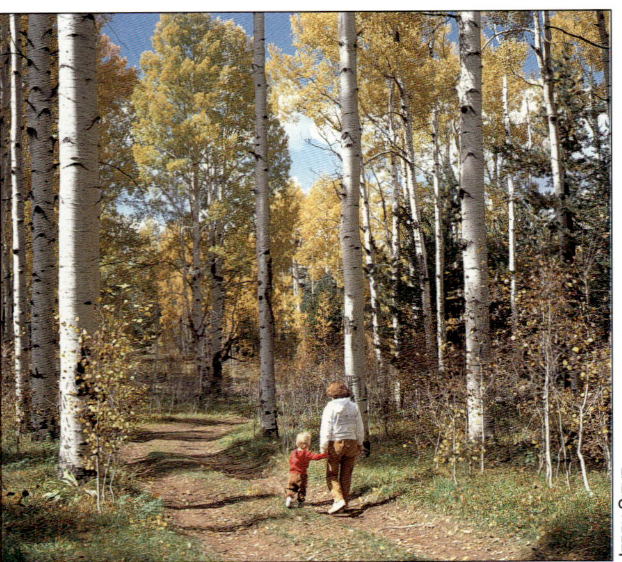
Jerry Sieve

terranean tunnel of total darkness. The cave is actually a lava tube which was formed when lava flowed down a canyon. The sides and top of the lava cooled and hardened as they came into contact with the rock and air. The interior of the flow remained hot and molten and when the source of the lava was cut off, the hot lava continued to flow out, leaving a flat-bottomed, round-roofed tunnel. A number of these tubes are scattered throughout the San Francisco Peaks Volcanic Field.

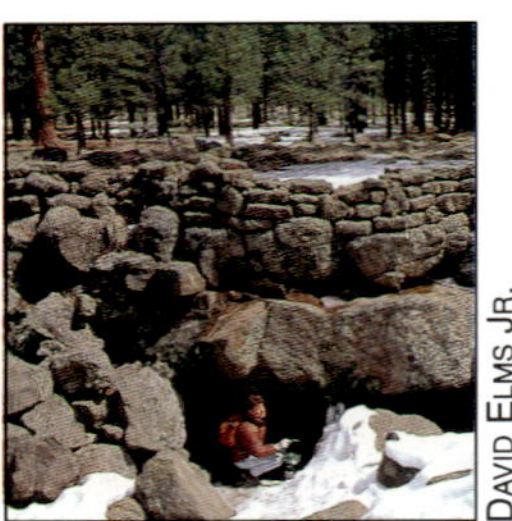
David Elms Jr.

Caution: Do not enter the cave unless you are prepared with the proper equipment: hiking shoes or boots, a hardhat (the tunnel is very low and narrow in places), and multiple flashlights, headlamps, or lanterns with extra batteries. Ice forms at the entrance so watch your step. And temperatures stay cold down under so wear warm clothing.

To return to Flagstaff, go back to Forest Road 245 and out to Highway 180. Turn right and 14 miles later you'll be in town.

its, partly because of its sacredness, and partly because the endangered San Francisco Peaks groundsel makes its home there.

To the Navajos, the San Francisco Peaks are one of four mountains that mark the boundaries of their land. They call them *Do'ko'oslid*. The most beautiful translation I have heard of that word is "abalone shell mountain." When fresh snowfall crowns the Peaks, they do gleam like abalone.

Navajo Frank Goldtooth, Jr., eloquently expressed the importance of the Peaks to the *Diné*: "this San Francisco Peak is . . . sitting there with prayers and it has white shell beads and turquoise and Apache tear drops and abalone, and that is what is sitting there with plants of life, sitting there with life."

The irresistible magnetism of these mountains has pulled people here for a long time. From the hazards and deprivations of the surrounding desert, the Peaks were an oasis; their melting snows bestowed water and their forested slopes yielded wood and game for food.

Spanish missionaries saw the Peaks from the Hopi mesas in 1629 and named them for Saint Francis of Assisi. Later, Anglo explorers commented on their "sublime summits" and "picturesque" scenery. Then, curiously, they named the individual peaks for people who had little or no association with them.

Mount Humphreys honors U.S. Army General Andrew Humphreys, who never set foot on the Peaks; Agassiz is named for Swiss zoologist Jean Louis Rodolphe Agassiz, who, likewise, was never here; and Fremont, for the "Pathfinder" John Charles Fremont, who, despite his several expeditions across the West, may have seen them from only as close as the town of Prescott.

Biologist C. Hart Merriam spent time on and around the Peaks beginning in July 1889. At a place called Little Spring, on the northwest side of the mountain near Hart Prairie, Merriam set up base camp in what he called "one of the grandest mountain counties in the world."

For two months, Merriam and his colleagues explored the San Francisco Peaks, Grand Canyon, and Painted Desert, cataloging the remarkable diversity of life he found within such a short distance in the region — desert, piñon-juniper woodland, ponderosa pines, fir and spruce forests, twisted bristlecone pines, and, at the highest elevations, alpine tundra. From that work, Merriam set forth a fundamental biological concept — the idea of life zones, biological communities determined by moisture and elevation.

As steadfast as the Peaks appear, they are in fact young upstarts on the landscape. About two million years ago, they weren't even here. But then the earth started to move. A succession of violent volcanic eruptions over the next million and a half years spewed out tremendous amounts of lava, cinders, and ash, which built up the San Francisco Peaks.

Since their fiery formation, the Peaks have been whittled down nearly 3,000 feet, mostly by water and ice. Three major glacial periods, from 200,000 to 11,000 years ago, were responsible for a good share of that trimming. On the north side of the Peaks, a 650-foot-thick glacier gouged out part of the wall of a collapsed volcanic crater, now called the Inner Basin, and piled up rock debris (moraines) as it crept down the mountainside. Though the glaciers are gone now, patches of snow persist in the highest reaches on the north side nearly year-round.

The Inner Basin is now part of the Kachina Peaks Wilderness, a 19,000-acre sanctuary that encompasses the highest reaches of the San Francisco Peaks. Protected within this mountain wilderness are forests,

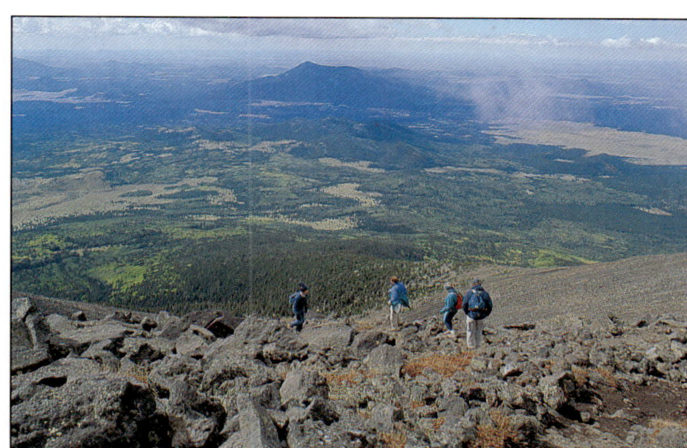

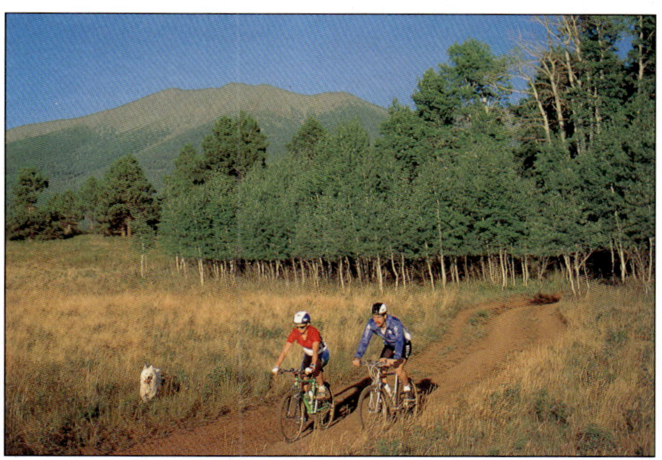

(TOP) *The view from the top of Humphreys Peak, 12,643 feet above sea level, is worth every step. On cloudless days hikers can easily see 200 miles in any direction.*
DON B. STEVENSON
(ABOVE) *A network of forest backroads outside the Kachina Peaks Wilderness is a mecca for mountain bikers, horseback riders, and four-wheel-drive enthusiasts.*
TOM BEAN

wildlife, sacred places, and silence. It's a place where Nature holds sway, where the elk, gopher, Clark's nutcracker, water pipit, wild turkey, dwarf shrew, candytuft, lupine, and even red algae find homes.

These life forms all need the wilderness, but so does Flagstaff, for it gives the town its water. Clouds gather in waves and ruffles around the tops of the Peaks. Those clouds drop snow and rain that soak into the volcanic rock and emerge as springs, life-giving water. Less tangible but no less important is the value of the wilderness as silent refuge, a place to go to restore the body and the spirit.

You can enter the roadless Kachina Peaks Wilderness only by foot power or horsepower (of the old-fashioned variety). U.S. routes 180 or 89 out of Flagstaff provide access to secondary roads that wind toward the wilderness. The Schultz Pass and Snowbowl roads off 180, along with several Forest Service roads, lead to trailheads. To get into the wilderness, try the Kachina, Weatherford, Aubineau, Bear Jaw, or Humphreys trails.

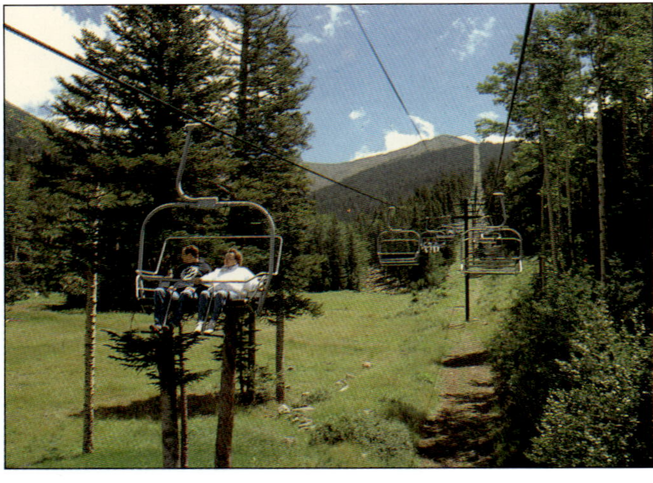

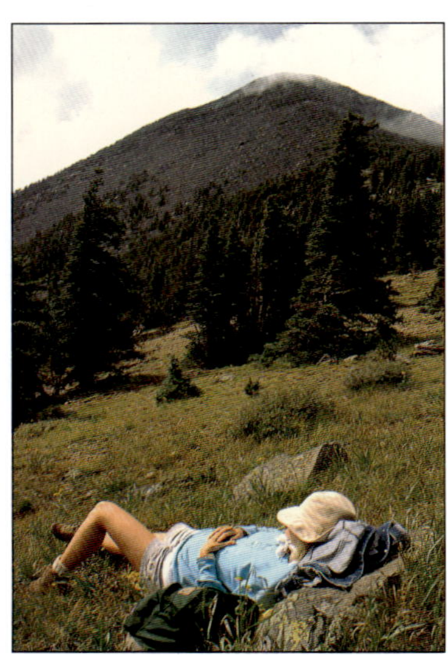

(ABOVE) *The skyride at the Arizona Snowbowl takes summer and autumn visitors close to the top of the San Francisco Peaks, with plenty of views along the way. Bring along a jacket as it is almost always windy and cool atop the Peaks.* FRANK ZULLO
(RIGHT) *A hiker takes a break on the San Francisco Peaks.* CHRISTINE KEITH

The most accessible route onto the Peaks is the Humphreys Trail. Take U.S. Highway 180 north out of Flagstaff seven miles and turn right onto the six-mile road up to the Arizona Snowbowl. The five-mile hiking trail starts at the base of the ski area.

During summer and fall you can take the Arizona Snowbowl Scenic Skyride. It offers stupendous views of the Peaks country from its highest point, 11,500 feet. Just buy a ticket at the lodge and hop on the 6,450-foot-long Agassiz chair lift. At the top you can get off, stretch your legs, and see the scenery before you ride back down. The skyride is open daily from mid June through Labor Day, and on weekends after Labor Day.

Judge John Weatherford wanted more people to see the San Francisco Peaks from the comfort of their Model T's and Model A's. Under the auspices of his San Francisco Boulevard Company, Weatherford carved a scenic — and daring — road through the Inner Basin to the top of the Peaks. He built the road from 1920 to 1926 and collected tolls from sightseers until 1934. Now closed to vehicles, the Weatherford Road has reverted to a beautiful hiking trail into the Inner Basin and up to the saddle between Agassiz and Humphreys.

Another way into the Inner Basin is via the Lockett Meadow Road (Forest Road 552) off U.S. Route 89. You can drive up three miles on this steep gravel road to a small camping area and the beginning of the Inner Basin Trail. The view of the Peaks from Lockett Meadow is astounding, the trail a pleasant uphill hike through pine, fir, and aspen. On a summer or fall day here, you may have good reason to believe you've reached heaven.

Please note: no mechanized vehicles, including mountain bikes, are permitted in the Kachina Peaks Wilderness. Also, a word of caution: go in the morning, for by noon on summer days anvil-topped clouds tower into the sky, and monsoon thunderstorms are likely. The top of the Peaks is no place to be if lightning is anywhere nearby. So watch the sky, and hustle down in short measure at any sign of thunder and lightning. And pack a sandwich, water, and a good wind and rain jacket.

A number of unpaved Forest Service roads also provide access to the high country. You can hike, horseback, or mountain bike on these roads and a number of backcountry trails; camp under the soughing pines; see the aspens in autumn; and ski, snowmobile, snowboard, or run a dog sled in winter.

In May, June, and early July, before the summer rains start, forests in northern Arizona become tinder dry. During high fire season, restrictions may be in place regarding campfires, smoking, off-highway vehicles, and chainsaws. During these dry times, the Forest Service issues warnings through the media and

The Arizona Snowbowl

When it comes to downhill skiing, I've always had an excuse — lift lines, neon-colored nylon, getting on and off the chairlift, cold feet. But with sufficient exhortation from my husband, I decided to try again, at the Arizona Snowbowl on the San Francisco Peaks.

It was a gorgeous February day — 55 inches of snow on the mountain, warm sunshine, and limitless visibility. At the appointed hour, I joined others for the "Ski Better" class. Instructor Paul Hubbard, a retired high school principal from Flagstaff, explained how his dad, Elmer, helped start the Snowbowl 50 years ago, when skis were seven-foot-long wooden boards with metal bindings called "bear traps."

After watching us try some turns down the hill, the instructors separated us into groups. I was placed in a group of one, which I suspect was not due to my superior ability. Jill Moore, a patient saint, took me under her wing. As we practiced turns for an hour or so, she advised me (probably in desperation) to pretend I was squashing a grape as I put my weight on my outside leg to execute a turn. I worked on that idea for a while as I followed Jill down the hill like a duckling following its mom.

By the end of the lesson, I'd gained some confidence and felt pretty good about my improved skiing ability. At least I hadn't done any face plants, broken any bones, or collided with another skier. And I really had fun.

Lest I mislead anyone, some people already *know* skiing is fun. They've been downhill skiing since they were six, and find the Snowbowl has plenty to offer — four chair lifts, 2,300 vertical feet, moguls galore, a variety of runs, including some fast steep ones above midway to challenge the most experienced, and a restaurant and bar at the lodge.

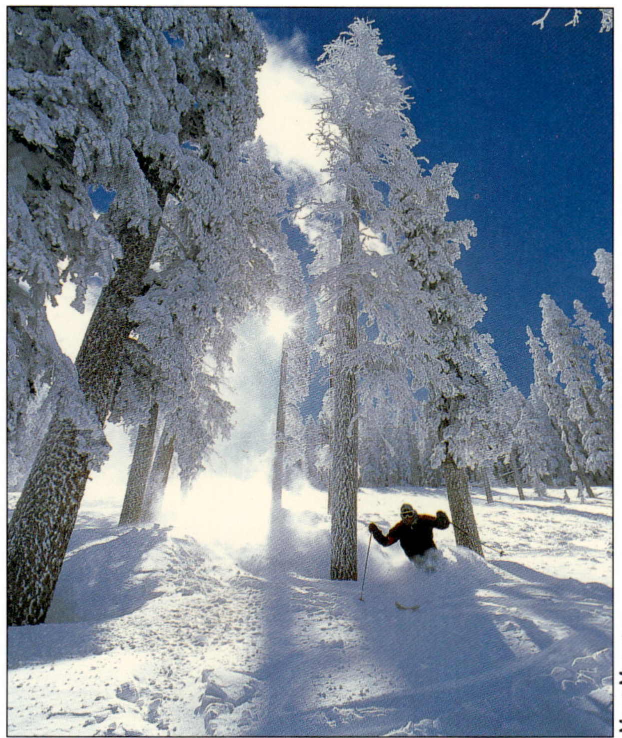
Marc Muench

posts fire danger signs throughout the Coconino and South Kaibab national forests. It is extremely important that these restrictions be observed by all forest users during these times.

Winter visits to the Peaks require special preparation and equipment to deal with the cold weather, snow and ice: cautious, common-sense driving and good tires, chains, or four-wheel-drive for icy and snow-packed roads; a shovel, matches, sleeping bag, extra food and water in the trunk; a change of warm, dry clothing; and a good sense of where you are and how far you've gone.

The days are short, and the weather can change from bright sunshine to howling blizzard at a moment's notice.

Whether you view the Peaks as a religious shrine, wilderness playground, biological wonderland, inspirational scenery, or all the above, they await your enjoyment just outside of Flagstaff.

When You Go

For information on camping, hiking, horseback riding, sightseeing, and winter sports around the San Francisco Peaks, contact:

Coconino National Forest
Supervisor's Office
2323 East Greenlaw Lane
Flagstaff, AZ 86004
(602) 527-3600

Arizona Snowbowl
P.O. Box 40
Flagstaff, AZ 86002
(602) 779-1951
For snow report, call: Flagstaff (602) 779-4577
Phoenix (602) 957-0404

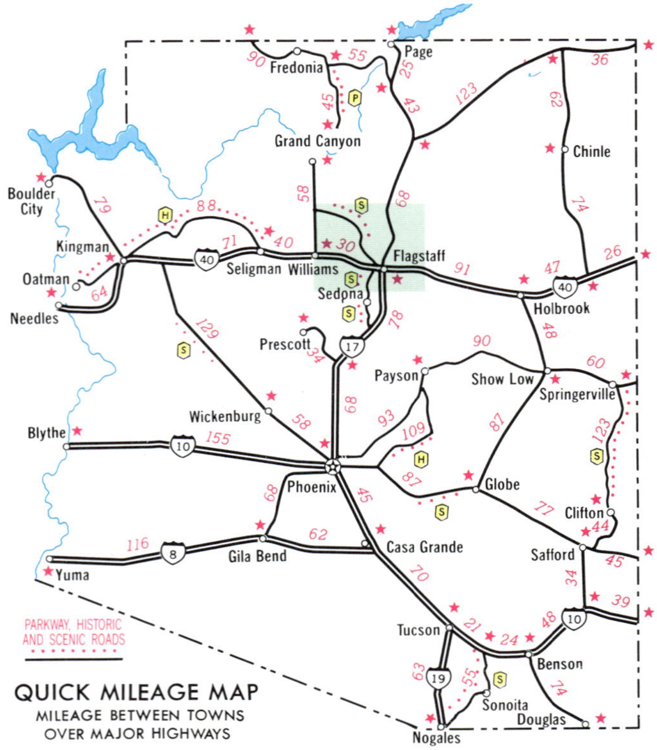

Maps designed by
Arizona Department of Transportation
Photogrammetry and Mapping Services

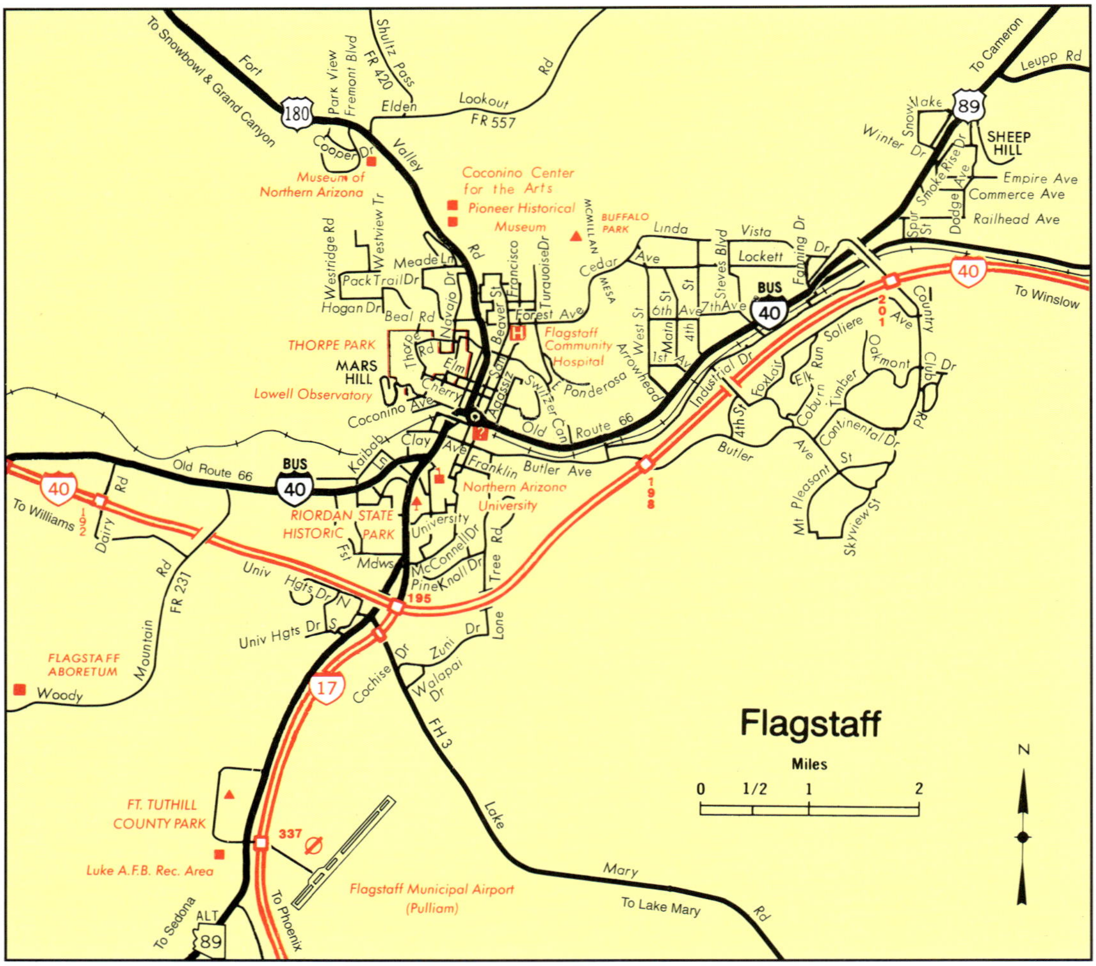

PARKWAY, HISTORIC AND SCENIC ROADS

QUICK MILEAGE MAP
MILEAGE BETWEEN TOWNS OVER MAJOR HIGHWAYS

Flagstaff

Miles
0 1/2 1 2

N

Peaks Area Legend

- 10 Interstate highway
- 95 U.S. route
- 85 State route
- 2 Indian reservation route
- Multilane divided highway
- Paved highway
- Gravel road
- Graded and drained
- Unimproved
- 5.7 Consolidated mileage
- Full traffic interchange
- Railroad
- Indian reservation
- National forest
- Parks and monuments
- Urbanized area
- Open water
- Live stream
- Intermittent stream
- County seat
- Municipal airport
- 500 foot contour lines
- ? Arizona tourist information
- Roadside rest area

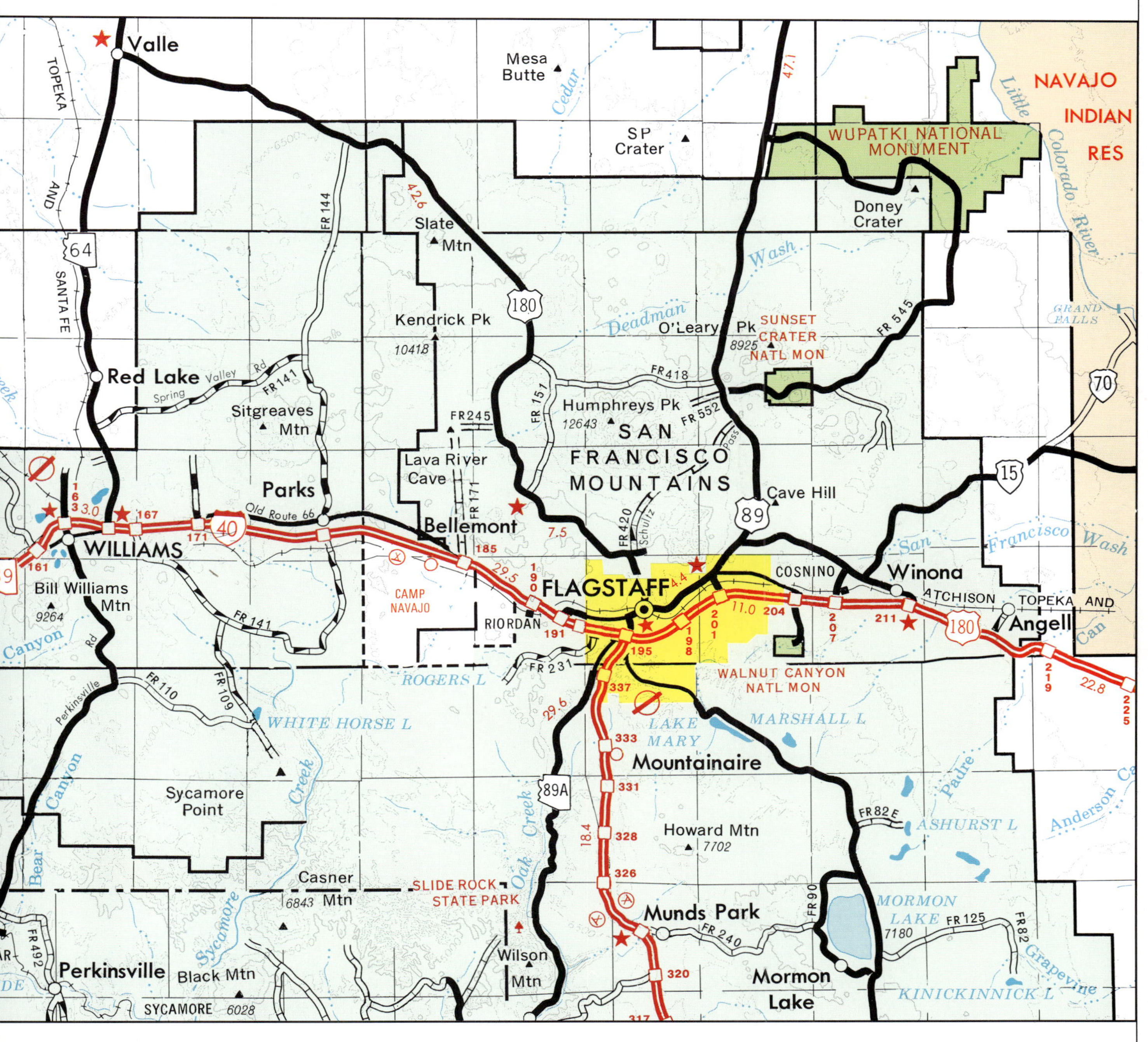

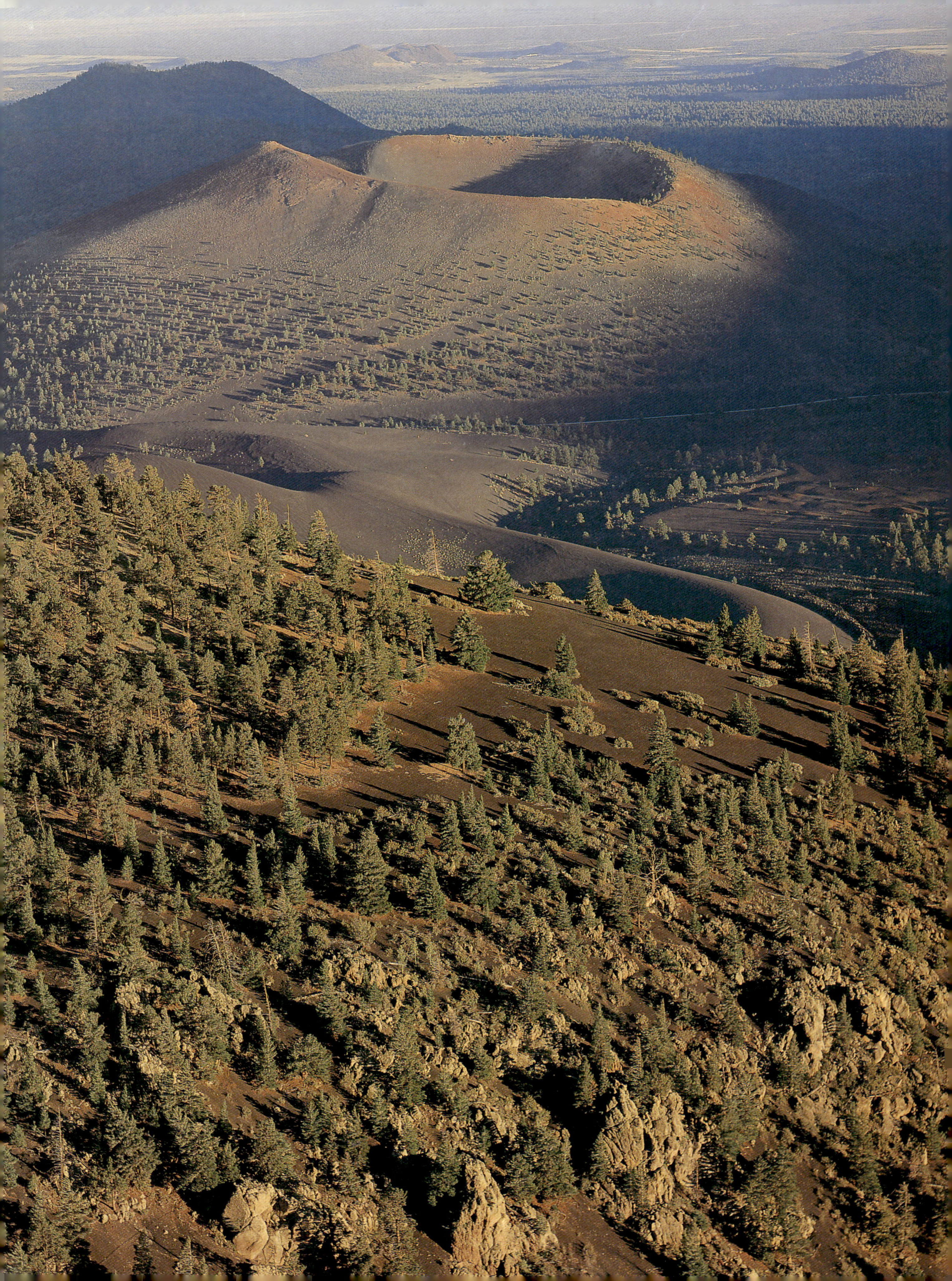

Chapter Three

North and East of the Peaks

Dormant Volcanoes and Vanished Cultures

Cinder cones surround Flagstaff, rising like dark islands from sunlit grasslands. Some cones are perfectly symmetrical, some not. Many have names: the well-known Sunset Crater, and the lesser-known SP, Strawberry, Colton, Roden, and others. Many hold small lakes ringed with aspens. Each is unique.

Geologically speaking, cinder cones are recent additions to the landscape of northern Arizona. Only about six million years ago volcanoes began to erupt sporadically in the region, eventually forming the 500 or so cones that punctuate the 2,000-square-mile San Francisco Volcanic Field.

Cinder cones are built when lava shoots out the vent of a volcano; as the eruptions continue, cinders, ash, pumice, and lapilli are blown into the air, cool, and settle back around the central vent, forming a cone of loose red, brown, and black rock.

(OPPOSITE PAGE) *The last rays of the sun ignite the rim of Sunset Crater, illustrating how this cinder cone earned its name.* JERRY SIEVE
(FOLLOWING PANEL, PAGES 36-37) *The solitary splendor of Wukoki Ruin at Wupatki National Monument speaks of a strong aesthetic sense among its prehistoric builders.* PETER KRESAN

From a raven's-eye view, another feature of cinder cones stands out — long, black tongues of basalt flow from the bases of some. If there isn't enough gas to send the boiling magma all the way out the top during an eruption, the liquid lava instead spills from a vent near the bottom of a cone and, hardening as it cools, forms these frozen rivers of stone.

From a distance the cones appear soft and inviting. Up close, it's a different story. The cinders are what geologists call "unconsolidated." Translated, that means walking on them is akin to walking on a field of ball bearings. And the sides of the cones are steep — their slopes are a consistent 33 degrees, the angle of repose of loose cinders. If you decide to hike up one, you'll soon be grinding into granny gear and making wide traverses to ease the pain on your hamstrings. But the views from their tops are spectacular, and the cones are often delightfully devoid of humanity.

Sunset Crater, one of the most beautiful of the cinder cones surrounding Flagstaff, rises to a thousand feet above the surrounding landscape. In A.D. 1064, a fissure, or crack in the earth, opened, ejecting fire-born rocks and glowing liquid lava. That eruption (and lesser ensuing ones for about the next 150 years) formed Sunset and other nearby craters and lava flows. The wonderful reds, yellows, purples, greens, and blacks that appear in the rock and give the crater

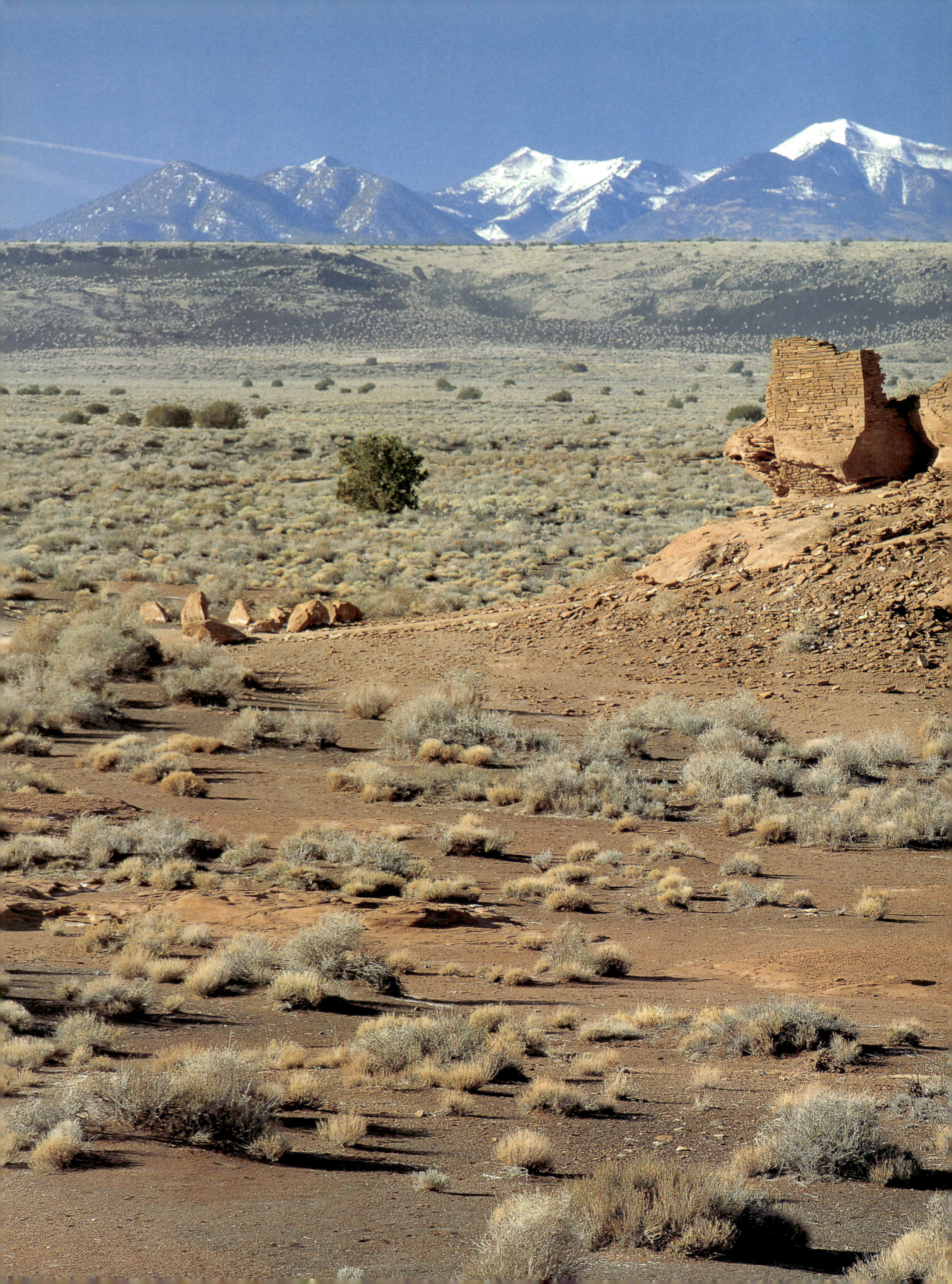

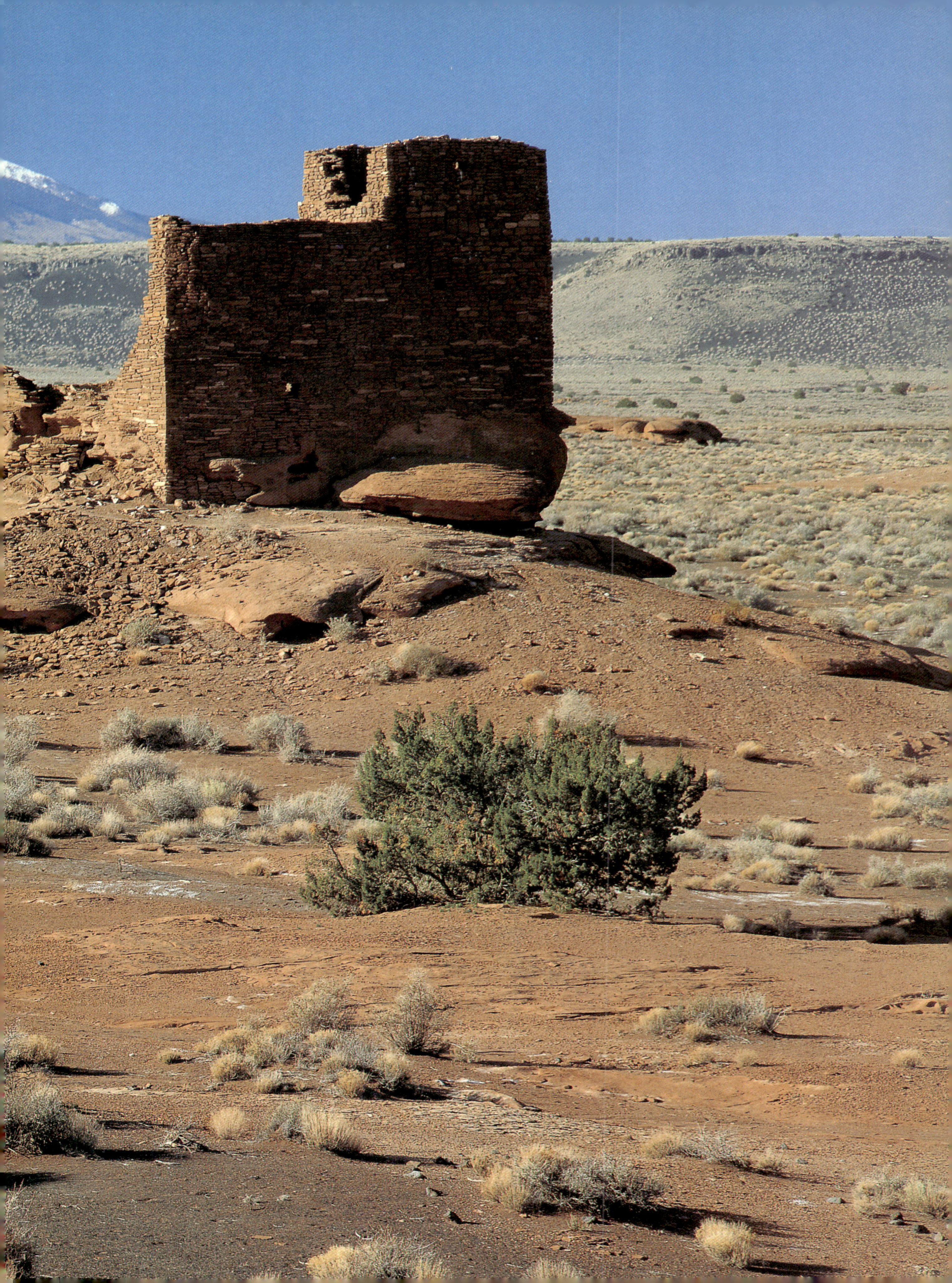

its name come from the presence of iron and other minerals in the original lava.

The Lava Flow Trail, a one-mile, self-guiding loop, follows the base of Sunset Crater and passes through part of the Bonito flow, but the trail up to the rim of Sunset Crater has been closed since the 1970s because of erosion.

The fires, hot ash, and deadly gases that spewed from Sunset Crater wreaked destruction upon the environment for a time. In 1930, archaeologists with the Museum of Northern Arizona discovered that people had been living in the Sunset Crater area at the time of its first eruption. The evidence was cinders and ashes resting directly on top of the burned timbers of a pithouse.

The Sinaguans who lived in the pithouse had been enjoying a peaceful farming life in the region for about four centuries. But in late 1064 or early 1065, they must have noticed a restlessness in the Earth because they packed up their belongings and left.

When the eruptions ceased, and with the new crater defining the landscape, the Sinagua people returned. Dr. Harold Colton, who named the Sinagua culture (Spanish for "without water"), believed the cinder mulch, the "black sand," held moisture and proved a boon to agriculture. He proposed that a land rush of sorts occurred after the Sunset Crater eruption with people coming from hundreds of miles around. His ideas have been modified in favor of evidence that a period of favorable rainfall may have encouraged farming, and that population growth may not have been as dramatic as Colton first estimated. Nevertheless, new people and new ways appeared in the area after the eruption: Hohokam from the south, the Cohonina from the west, and Anasazi from the north and east.

Amid the red sandstone and golden grasslands 22 miles north of Sunset Crater, Wupatki National Monument preserves and interprets a community that archaeologists speculate was for a time one of the great crossroads and a cultural melting pot of the prehistoric Southwest. There the Sinaguans built numerous pueblos, field houses, and ceremonial ball courts.

The namesake pueblo, Wupatki, is a multistory, above-ground dwelling built of sandstone masonry in the style of the Anasazi. Some of the ponderosa timbers used in the pueblo were from trees that may have

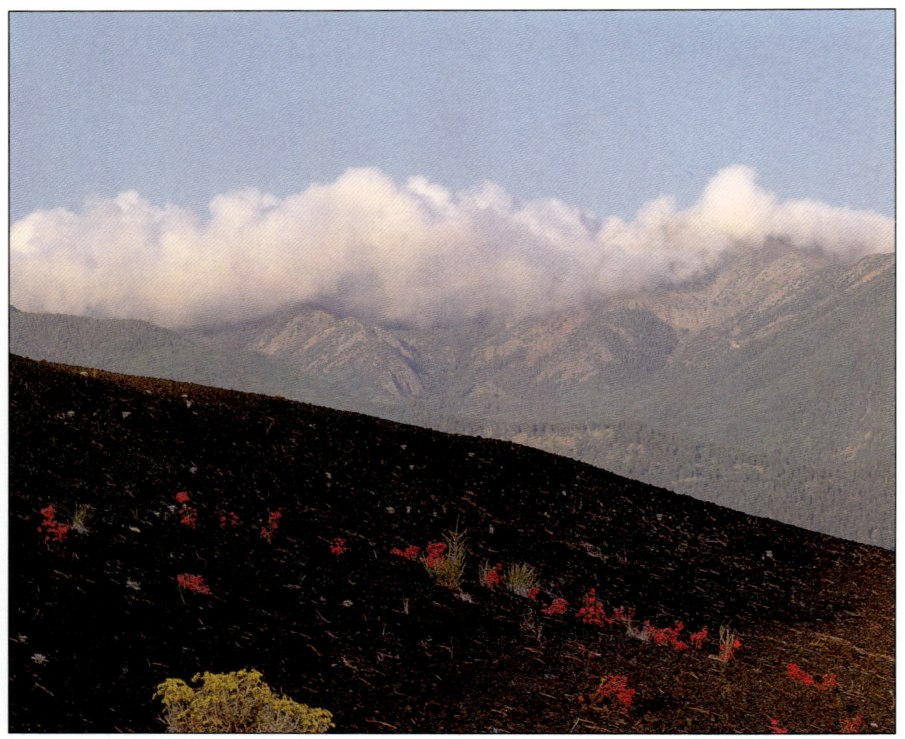

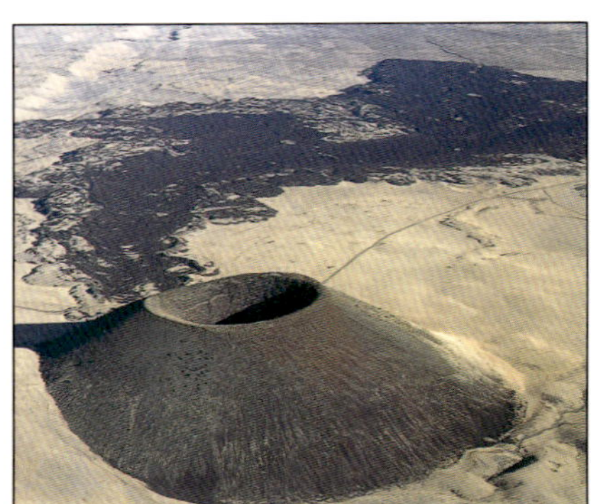

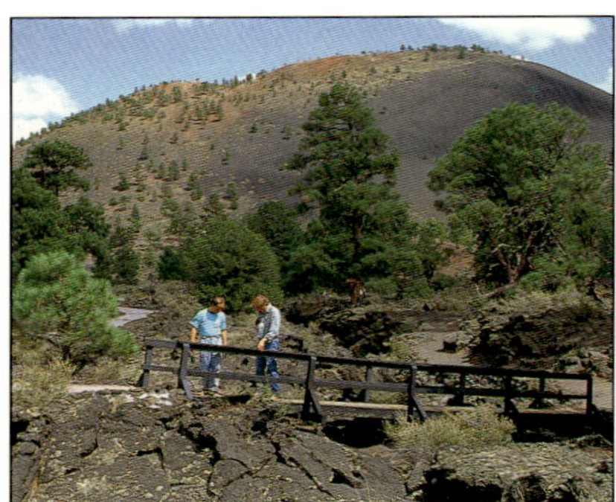

(CLOCKWISE FROM ABOVE) *The slopes of a basaltic cinder cone support only a few plants adapted to the tough environment of the San Francisco Volcanic Field.* ROBERT MCDONALD
An aerial view of SP Crater graphically shows the lava that flowed from the base of the volcano. PETER KRESAN
Along the Lava Flow Nature Trail, visitors to Sunset Crater Volcano National Monument can obtain closeup views of the fascinating structures of the Bonito Lava Flow. JAMES TALLON

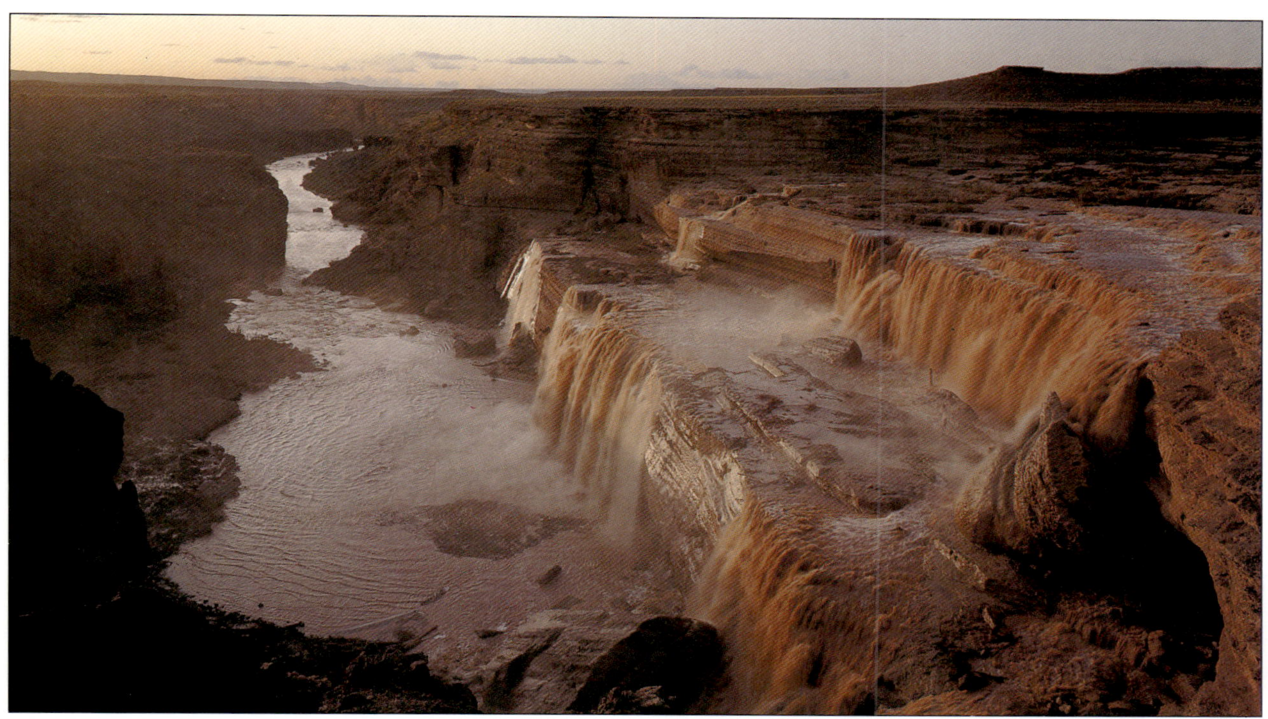

Les Manevitz

Back road to Grand Falls

"The Grand Falls of the Little Colorado River are staging their annual spring spectacle east of Flagstaff." The seasonal flowing of Grand Falls became newsworthy early on. Flagstaff's newspaper, the *Arizona Daily Sun,* ran this item in its columns 25 years ago.

One Saint Patrick's Day we decided to make a pilgrimage to see if the spectacle was taking place. By mid-March, daytime temperatures usually have warmed enough to melt snow in the White Mountains in eastern Arizona, the headwaters of the Little Colorado River, and deliver the muddy water that cascades over the falls.

For much of its course the Little Colorado winds at leisure through a broad, flat, sandy valley. But at Grand Falls the river tumbles purposefully over a terrace of rock 185 feet high. This day, the water rushed down in three broad ribbons like sand pouring through the fingers of someone's hand. Bewitched, I breathed the mist from the muddy river brew.

As Harold Colton so well told, the "chocolate Niagara" of Grand Falls originated when a nearby volcano sent out a "stream of basalt, glowing and steaming. Reaching the canyon rim, it plunged as a fiery cataract into the river, blocking the course of the stream." That lava dam backed up a lake nearly all the way to Winslow about 150,000 years ago.

The lake has long ago filled with silt, but you can still clearly see the black lava on the west bank of the falls. From an aerial perspective, you also could see how the Little Colorado meandered around that lava tongue and spilled back into the canyon beyond the dammed area, resuming its former path to meet with the mother stream, the Colorado River at the bottom of the Grand Canyon. Thus Grand Falls was born. Though dry or flowing at just a trickle most of the year, the Little Colorado is sometimes flooded by spring runoff and summer thunder storms making Grand Falls grand indeed.

Getting there: To see the falls, drive out U.S. Route 89 to the Camp Townsend-Winona Road. Turn right (east) and continue eight miles to the Leupp Road. Turn left (northeast) and proceed another 15 miles to the boundary of the Navajo Nation. Turn left (north) onto Navajo Route 70 and go nine miles on this good graveled road to the falls. There is little to warn you that you've reached the river, until you're *there,* at the edge. To the left a cindered road heads down to some picnic ramadas which afford spectacular views on the brink of the falls.

Caution: While most cars can make the trip to Grand Falls most of the time, a high clearance vehicle is best. In wet weather, stretches of the road are impassable even for four-wheel-drive vehicles.

grown at nearby Sunset Crater.

A self-guiding trail leads through Wupatki Pueblo, inhabited during the classic period of the Sinagua, from around A.D. 1100 to 1225. Also at Wupatki Pueblo are a Hohokam-style ballcourt, a huge amphitheater, and a blowhole, a naturally occurring hole in the earth that responds to changing atmospheric pressures, variously drawing air in and blowing it out. The Indian interpretation is that this is where Mother Earth breathes.

Along the drive through the monument you can view other ruins including Wukoki, Lomaki, Nalakihu, and Citadel. As you marvel at these elegant buildings, you may look beyond them and well wonder how the Sinagua managed to survive in this land that indeed appears almost devoid of running water. There were a few springs in the area, such as at Wupatki, but mainly the people had to be ingenious, capturing runoff water in rock depressions after rains, and from streams that flowed intermittently.

I never tire of the view from the top of Doney Mountain, a crater named for irascible Ben Doney, a Civil War veteran and early farmer, rancher, prospector, and political gadfly in the Flagstaff area. To the east and south, the land steps down to the Little

(FACING PAGE) *Hardy ponderosa pine trees dot the cinder-covered landscape of the Bonito Lava Flow at Sunset Crater. The flow was part of the eruption of the crater in A.D. 1064.*
DAVID W. LAZAROFF

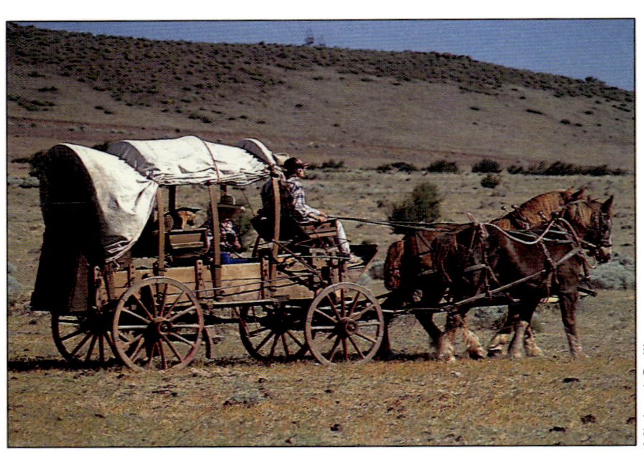
Michael Collier

HISTORIC GRAND CANYON STAGE ROUTE

George Yard hitched up the "girls," Maude and Penny, to his covered wagon. Though the two draft horses didn't know it, they were about to embark on a real journey. It was Memorial Day weekend, 1991. George and Sharon Yard had invited my husband and me to join them on a trip on the old Grand Canyon stage road. George is a long-time Flagstaff physician and Sharon is his nurse. Medicine is their profession, but ranching is in their blood, and they love nothing more than to put on old western garb, pull the wagon out of the barn, and go for a ride.

This ride on the Grand Canyon stage route would be the farthest they had ever taken Maude and Penny. Sharon Yard's brother, Tuba City postmaster Lindell Cornelison, joined us, driving his wagon pulled by two handsome mules, Kit and Ruby. With a host of family and friends in the wagons and on horseback, we struck out on a reconnaissance for the following year's centennial commemoration of the stage route.

From 1892 to 1901, passengers boarded stages at the Bank Hotel in Flagstaff for the 12-hour, 65-mile ride to the Canyon. The stages went out through Fort Valley, stopped for relays at Fern Mountain Ranch in Hart Prairie, then headed north past Babbitt's Cedar Ranch to Moqui Station and finally to Grandview Point. (On our trip we started at Kendrick Park, took a slower pace, and arrived at the Grand Canyon in four days.)

A short time after we got underway, Lindell Cornelison stopped to fix the iron tire that was separating from the wooden wagon wheel. Later, we had to retrieve stray items that fell beside the trail when the chuck box bounced open. Besides those two minor mishaps, the whole trip went smoothly. There were moments along the way when I felt transported a hundred years back in time.

The second night out, camped at the base of Mesa Butte, we dined on delicious fry bread that Lindell Cornelison's wife, Mary, made over a juniper fire. We stopped for lunch the next day at historic Moqui Stage Stop where the road climbs back up into the forest. We spent our last night out at Russell Tank beneath a gibbous moon. The following morning, we made a notable procession out to Grandview Point, where, a hundred years earlier, stage passengers had their first view of the great gorge.

Now most of the old Grand Canyon stage route is negotiable by passenger vehicle or mountain bike on a series of Forest Service roads. The stage route is part of the 700-mile Arizona Trail that runs from the Mexico border to Utah.

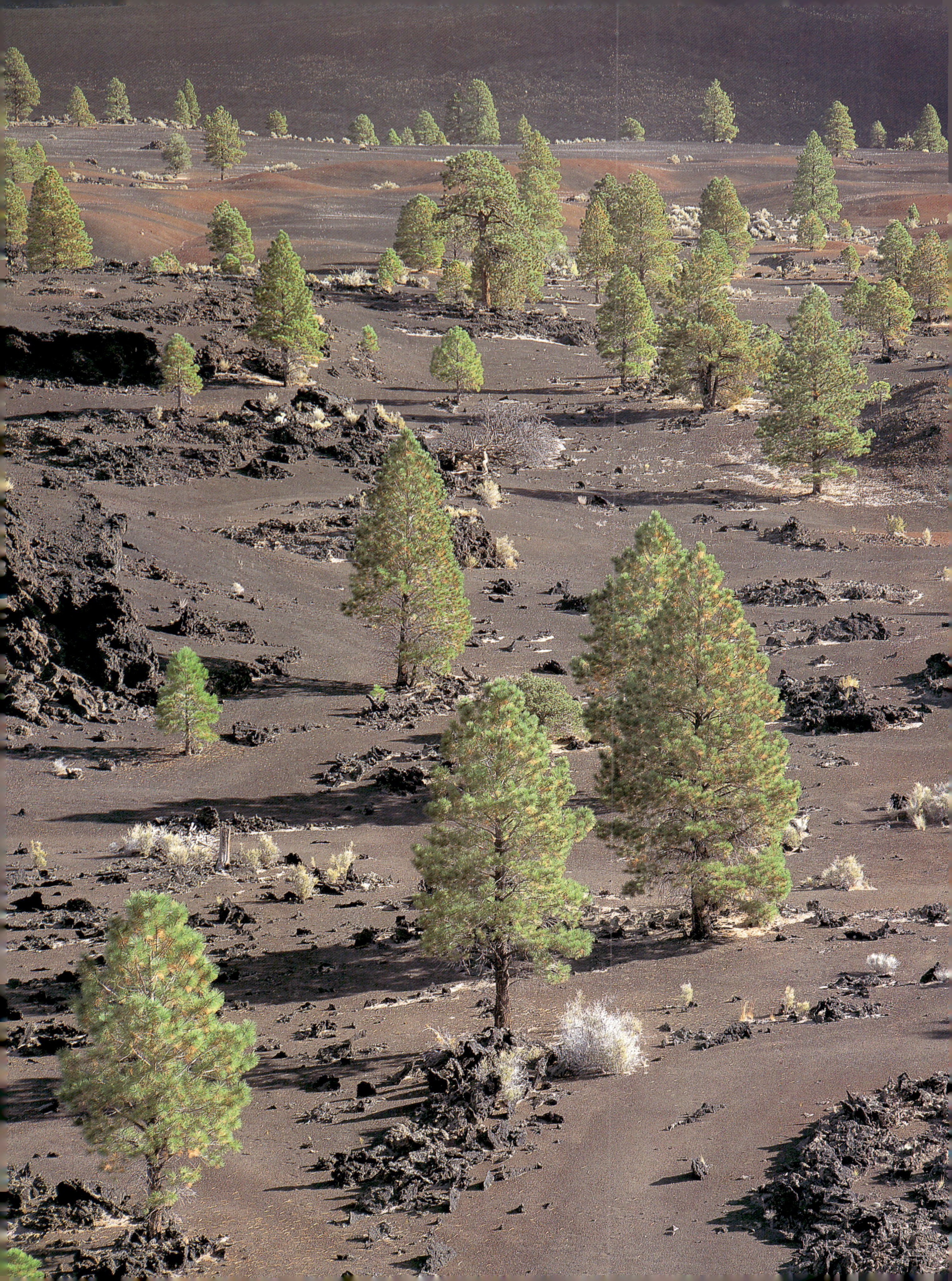

Colorado River, then stretches seemingly forever into the Painted Desert and to the Hopi Buttes. To the west rise Gray Mountain and SP Crater; to the south, the San Francisco Peaks and Sunset Crater.

The 1/2-mile trail up Doney Crater is on Forest Service land. To reach it, take U.S. Route 89 north out of Flagstaff for 30 miles. Just past Antelope Hills, turn right (east) at the Wupatki entrance. Go nine miles. Turn right at the Viewpoint and Lunch Area sign, and park at the picnic grounds. The trailhead is marked.

When I arrived one spring day, the air was absolutely still. No people. No wind. I started up the trail, my boots crunching in the soft cinders. Drought-resistant plants such as Mormon tea, Apache plume, and rabbitbrush lined the trail. Halfway up, something flashed in the corner of my eye. Four pronghorns bounded silently across the base of the crater, then stopped to graze the shrubs. I, too, stopped in my tracks, transfixed by their gracefulness. The cinder cones, which at times seem devoid of life, can offer other wildlife surprises, too. One frequenter of the cone country has told me of seeing foxes, porcupines, and even a mountain lion with her cub.

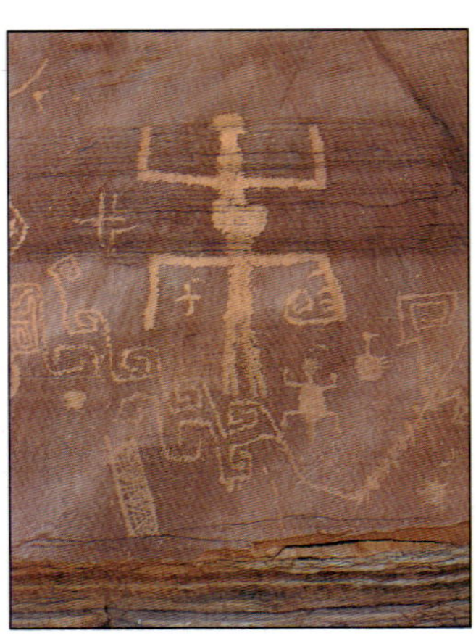

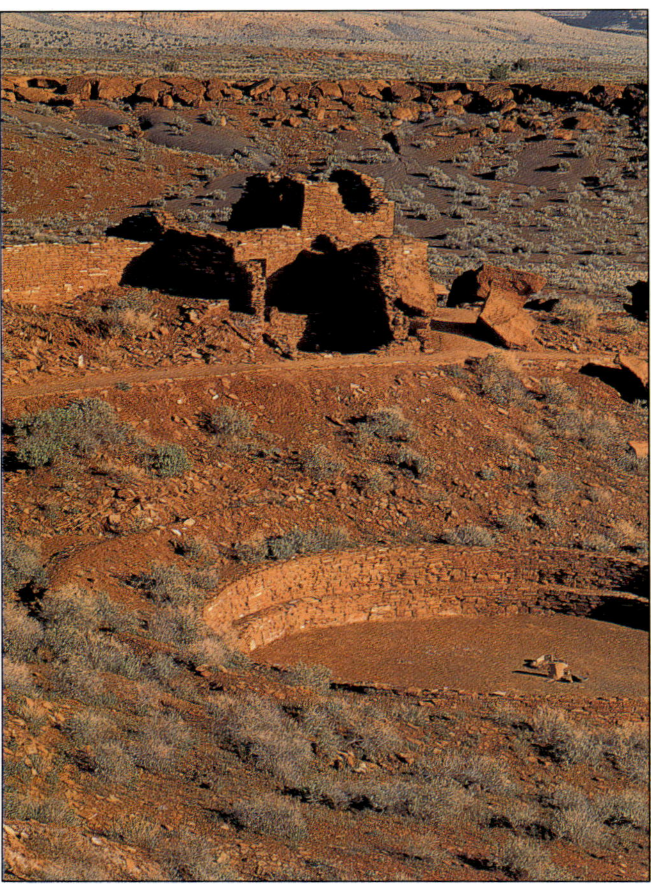

The trail branches, one leading left to Little Doney Crater, the other right to Big Doney. I followed one, then the other, seeing along the way rock outlines of fieldhouses and small farmsteads of the Sinagua. Might the Sinagua have been living here when Sunset Crater erupted? What a fireworks show they would have seen.

The Sinagua also settled in a beautiful limestone enclave southeast of Flagstaff, now set aside as Walnut Canyon National Monument. Outside the visitors center you'll see hardy souls stopping to catch their breath. They have just come up the 240 steps on the Island Trail that drops 185 feet into Walnut Canyon and loops around an "island" (more accurately a peninsula) of rock.

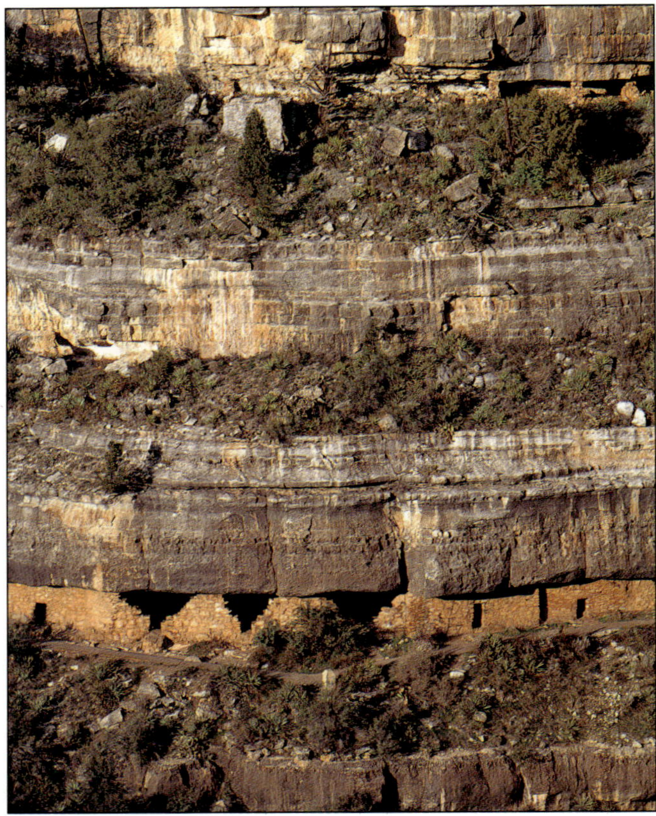

(ABOVE LEFT) *The prehistoric inhabitants of Wupatki National Monument chipped enigmatic symbols into the burnished surfaces of the rock cliffs.* DAVID H. SMITH

(LEFT) *Residents of Wupatki Pueblo may have gathered in the circular amphitheatre for ceremonies or dances.* MICHAEL COLLIER

(ABOVE) *The Sinagua Indians of Walnut Canyon knew how to utilize passive solar warmth in their high-elevation homes.* ROBERT MCDONALD

Along the trail you can get a close look at the homes of people who lived in Walnut Canyon about 800 years ago. Archaeologists speculate that the Sinagua who settled here did so because of overcrowding elsewhere in the region. In this canyon they eked out a living by farming the creek bottom and the surrounding rim of the canyon for 150 years.

As I descended the trail I marveled at the fresh green leaves on the Gambel oaks. Hummingbirds, just back from wintering in the southern hemisphere, dive-bombed me and filled the air with their metallic whirrings. White, waxy blossoms hung from yucca stalks. Deep crimson chalices adorned claretcup cacti, and garish red Indian paintbrush and carmine thistles splashed color on the rock slopes. An incredible profusion of plants grows in Walnut Canyon — snowberry, barberry, wolfberry, elderberry, hoptree, currant, sumac, juniper, piñon, wild grape, and black walnut. All provided food, fuel, or medicine for the Sinagua.

Besides the wild things they collected, the Sinagua farmed the canyon's rims by building rock dams across even the smallest washes to hold back water and gather soil for corn fields. Corn was the staple of their diet. (An exhibit in the visitor center says the average Sinaguan ate three quarts of corn meal a day.)

Sinaguan homes fit intimately into the canyon environment. With native stone and mortar they enclosed many snug alcoves and overhangs to create rooms. You can still crouch to see these small living rooms, the walls sooted black from their cooking fires, and ancient fingerprints still visible in the clay mortar.

Across the canyon are more such rooms tucked into the honeycombed limestone walls — as many as 300 of them in all in Walnut Canyon, grouped into more than 80 distinct cliff dwellings. Such groupings intrigue archaeologists. Studying patterns of settlement, they are learning how prehistoric people organized themselves, how they made decisions, and something of the rituals they might have practiced. Clay figurines, prayer feathers, and turquoise beads found here hint at symbolism and beliefs that went beyond sheer survival for the Sinagua.

After circling the island, I started back up the steps. There *may* be 240 of them — I lost count along the way. I was sweating and welcomed the bench near the top of the trail. Later, as I cooled down and ate lunch along the Rim Trail, I watched hawks soaring on the wind over Walnut Canyon.

To reach Walnut Canyon National Monument, take I-40 east from Flagstaff to Exit 204. Drive south on Walnut Canyon Road to the monument. The Island Trail is just under a mile round trip. The Rim Trail is a flat, three-quarter-mile path. Both are asphalt surfaced. The monument opens at 8:00 a.m. Trails close at 4:30, and the gates to the parking lot are locked at 5:00 p.m. each day.

Several weekends each year, the public is welcome to visit Elden Pueblo on the eastern edge of Flagstaff. A public archaeology program operates at this prehistoric site giving anyone who is interested a chance to excavate under the supervision of professional archaeologists. Elden is a 70-room pueblo that was a central Sinaguan site during the 11th century. Public dig days are free — all you need is sunscreen, a brown-bag lunch, and a desire to learn. The site is located northeast of town on U.S. Route 89. For information contact Elden Pueblo Archaeology Project, P.O. Box 3496, Flagstaff 86003; (602) 527-3475.

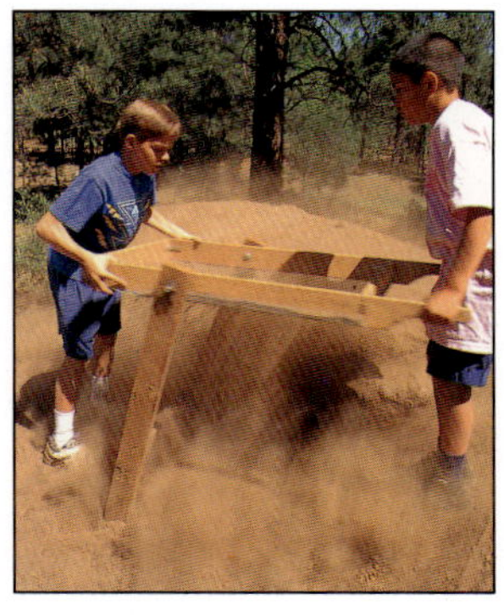

Volunteers sift for artifacts at Elden Pueblo. PETER NOEBELS

WHEN YOU GO

Coconino National Forest
Supervisor's Office
2323 East Greenlaw Lane
Flagstaff, AZ 86004
(602) 527-3600

Walnut Canyon National Monument
Walnut Canyon Road
Flagstaff, AZ 86004
(602) 526-3367
Open daily except Christmas.
Admission fee charged.

Sunset Crater Volcano National Monument
Route 3, Box 149
Flagstaff, AZ 86002
(602) 556-7042

Wupatki National Monument
HC 33, Box 444A
Flagstaff, AZ 86004
(602) 556-7040

Wupatki and Sunset Crater Volcano national monuments are open year-round except Christmas Day. Admission fee. Camping is available in summer at the Forest Service's Bonito Campground near the Sunset Crater visitors center.

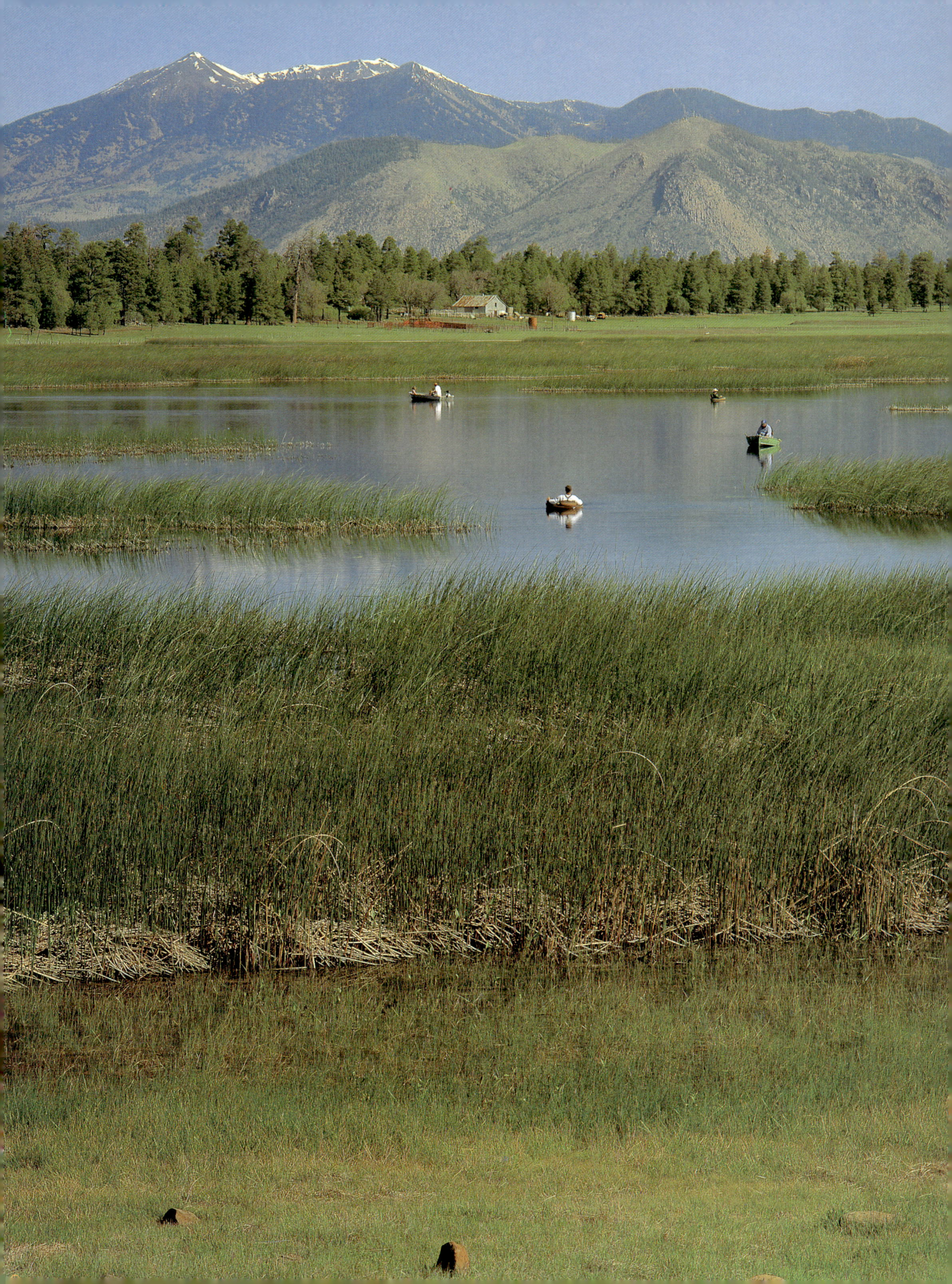

Chapter Four

Southeast of the Peaks

A Land of Lakes Attracting Wildlife and Outdoor Enthusiasts

South of Flagstaff on Anderson Mesa sits tiny Marshall Lake, given over to waterfowl and fishermen in small boats or float tubes. One perfect Sunday morning in June, we took our newly purchased sea kayak to Marshall to try it out.

Immediately upon launching, we were greeted by the teeming life of the marshy lake. American coots were breeding, their nests of cut cattail stalks floating on the water. The calls of the yellow-headed blackbirds were like the sound of wind blowing in venetian blinds. We saw eared grebes, a pair of great blue herons, and an osprey wheeling overhead. Water snails clung tenaciously to the cattails, and dragonflies lighted on our bow. I could hardly believe I was in Arizona.

Lakes are a rare pleasure in this dry state. Several are set like jewels in the basalt-capped plateau south of Flagstaff. Lake Mary Road (Forest Highway 3) south of Flagstaff provides scenic access to most of them — including Marshall, Lake Mary, Mormon, Kinickinnick, and Ashurst.

Five-thousand-acre Mormon Lake is the largest natural lake in Arizona. Standing at the overlook beside the lake, I try to imagine what Antonio de Espejo may have thought when he was here in 1583. He and his Spanish entourage had traversed the south side of the lake en route to the Verde Valley. But despite the stunning view of the San Francisco Peaks, Espejo did not linger. He was searching for gold, not scenery.

Nearly three centuries would pass before any pioneers really settled at Mormon Lake, and they gave the place its name. In 1878, Latter-day Saints started a dairy on the west shore of the lake to supply butter and cheese to their settlements in the Little Colorado River valley. They also relocated an entire sawmill here from Mount Trumbull on the Arizona Strip. The site was called Millville.

For a brief time, it looked like Mormon Lake might be a bustling stop on a new rail line. In 1887, the Atlantic & Pacific Railroad started building south of Flagstaff to connect with the Mineral Belt Railroad. The grand plan was for the line to serve the rich copper mines near Globe, but it was never finished. The railroad grade did get as far as Mormon Lake, where more than a hundred tons of wool awaited shipment.

The shimmering lake supported resort and tour boat operations in the 1930s. Now, though, during long dry spells the shallow lake dries up. When water is sufficient, the marshes that line the lake are filled with the jungle-like sounds of waterfowl. Great blue herons lift off the lake at dusk, and a fresh hatch of insects swirls in clouds in the air.

When Mormon Lake is low it is weedy and hard to fish, but there are plentiful bullheads and northern

(OPPOSITE PAGE) *The quiet waters of Marshall Lake south of Flagstaff draw anglers, who may come as much for the spectacular view of the San Francisco Peaks as for the fishing.* BOB TREHEARNE

(FOLLOWING PANEL, PAGES 46-47) *Upper Lake Mary, flanked by Mormon Mountain, provides plenty of recreational opportunities within a short drive of Flagstaff.* PETER NOEBELS

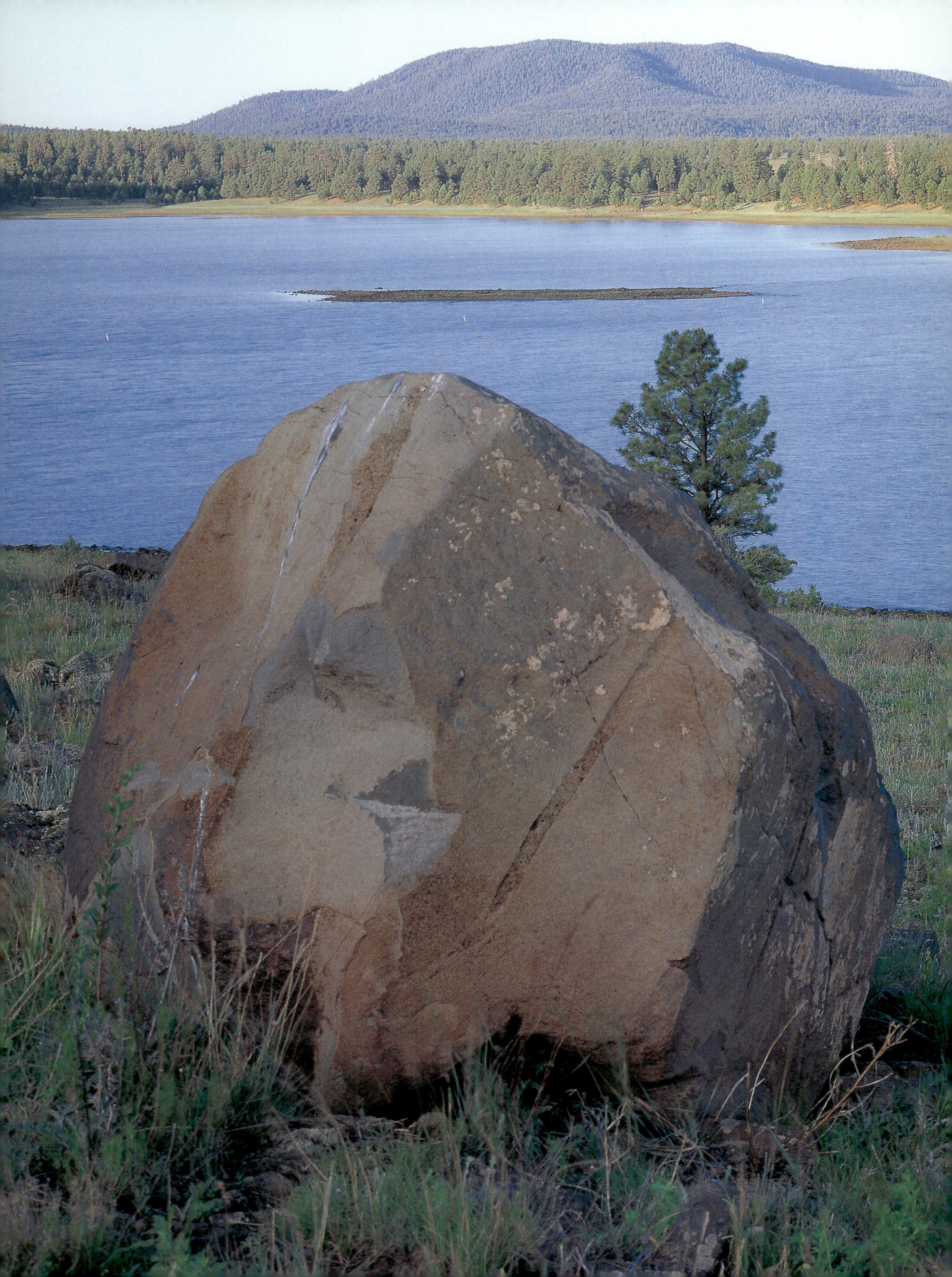

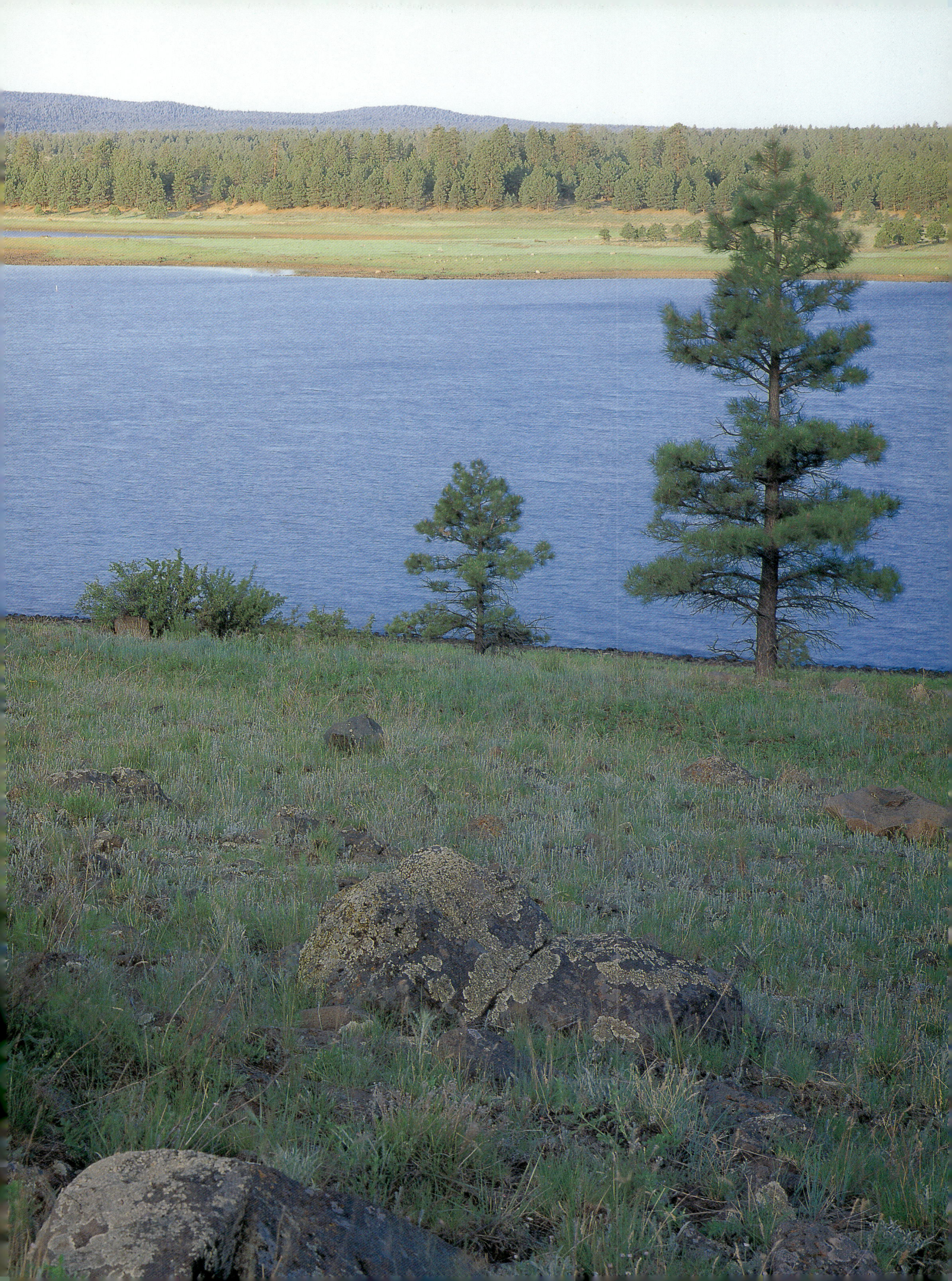

pike, including some big ones.

Nearby Lake Mary is an artificial lake, dammed at the turn of the century by Tim Riordan who named the lake for his daughter. Actually two lakes, Upper and Lower Lake Mary are a major water supply for Flagstaff. At the first hint of spring, boaters, fishermen, and water skiers flock to her waters.

Long, narrow, 600-acre Upper Lake Mary offers anglers northern pike, walleye, and catfish. Local fishermen tell me pike will hit anything shiny such as spoons or wobbling plugs, and that they've also had good luck catching all three species with cut bait such as waterdogs, smelt, or anchovy. Lower Lake Mary at only 100 acres is often likely to be low and unfishable. When it does have water, it holds the same species as the upper lake.

Herds of elk frequent the lake country and are seen — and more often heard when the males bugle during the fall rut. Elk live in the ponderosa forest in summer and early fall, then migrate down to the piñon-juniper woodland in winter. Wild turkeys strut across the open meadows near water, and bald eagles overwinter along the lakes, perching in tall snags and hooking fish in open waters. Osprey nest in big ponderosas on the shores of lakes Mary, Marshall, and Ashurst, diving to capture fish in their huge talons. When the osprey are nesting, boaters are requested not to disturb the birds by landing on shore or walking near nest areas.

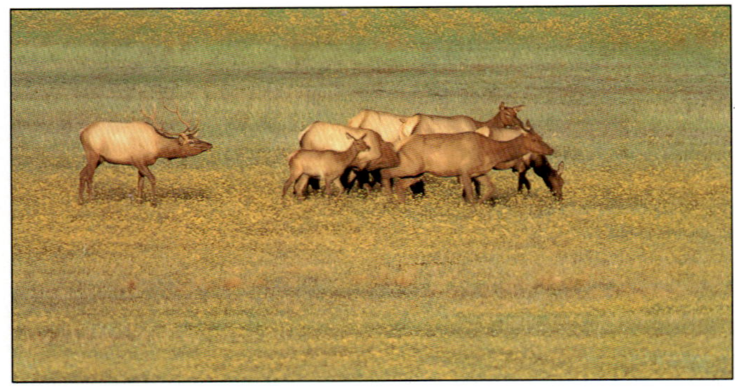

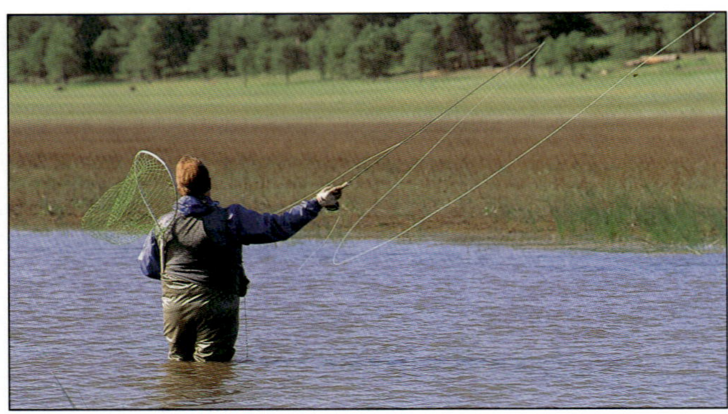

(TOP) *A bull elk herds his harem across a flowered meadow near Mormon Lake.* FRANK ZULLO
(ABOVE) *Anglers cast for the trout that thrive in the lakes of northern Arizona.* PETER NOEBELS
(OPPOSITE PAGE) *With the Peaks on the horizon, campers enjoy a tranquil twilight at Ashurst Lake, a trout fishery.* BOB AND SUZANNE CLEMENZ

Some of the plateau lakes, such as Marshall, have resulted when natural craters and depressions in the basalt cap rock filled with runoff. Others, including Ashurst and Kinickinnick lakes and Lake Mary, have been created by dams. Ashurst and Kinnickinnick were built specifically for trout fisheries.

At 200 acres, Ashurst is the area's most popular lake. Pan-sized rainbow trout and an occasional brook trout are the fare there. Fall fishing is best because in summer the lake's water gets warm and you have to troll deep to find the trout.

To reach the big brown trout and medium-sized rainbows at Kinickinnick Lake you have to travel Forest Roads 124 and 82, which at times can be rough. But it is worth it for fall fly fishing, and trolling anytime.

All the lakes can be reached on forest roads. All have boat docks and ramps, some of which are paved, and some of which are dirt and gravel. Lake Mary is open to water skiing, with no restrictions on motor sizes. On most others, motor size is limited to eight horsepower, or motors are not advised because of shallow water.

Cross-country skiers of all abilities flock to Mormon Lake Village in winter. The Mormon Lake Ski Touring Center grooms about 20 miles of trails along the lake and on the slopes of Mormon Mountain. Snowmobiling and ice fishing are also possible in winter.

Developed Forest Service campgrounds are located at several of the rim lakes: Double Springs and Dairy Springs by Mormon Lake, Lake View and Pine Grove at Lake Mary, and Ashurst Lake and Forked Pine at Ashurst. The closest facilities are at the small settlement of Mormon Lake Village ("Population 50 to 5,000" says the sign) with a lodge, restaurant, and ski and other equipment rentals available.

WHEN YOU GO

Coconino National Forest
Supervisor's Office
2323 East Greenlaw Lane
Flagstaff, AZ 86004
(602) 527-3600

Kaibab National Forest
Supervisor's Office
800 South 6th Street
Williams, AZ 86046
(602) 635-8200

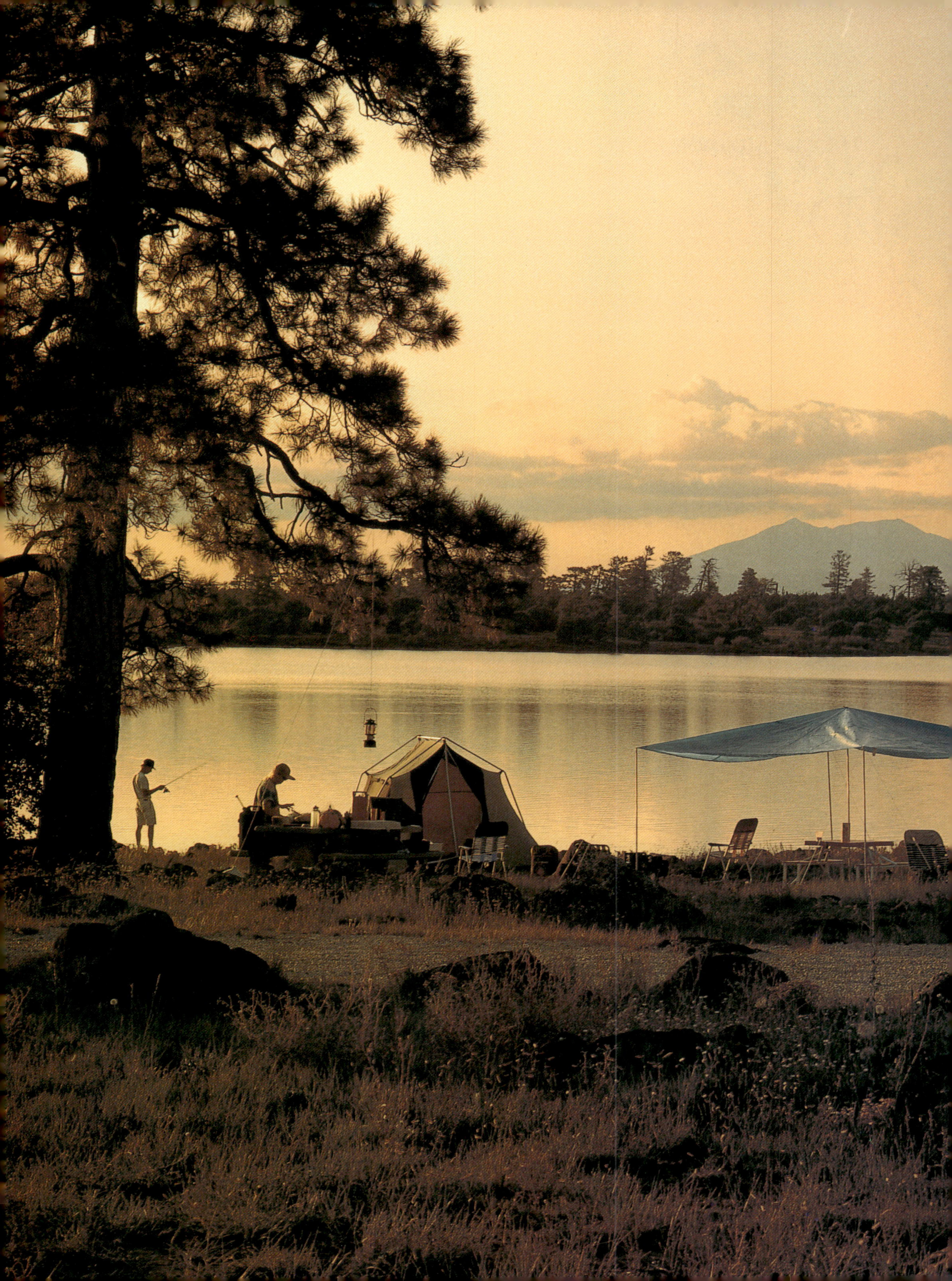

Hike up Mormon Mountain

Dairy Springs Campground is quiet this August morning. I find the Forest Service sign that marks the beginning of the trail up Mormon Mountain. This three-mile trail climbs 1,500 feet to the top of the 8,456-foot-high mountain. Along the way, I pass through an old-growth ponderosa forest inhabited by brown creepers, pygmy nuthatches, wild turkeys, owls, and goshawks.

The trail heads uphill at a fairly good grade. I notice I'm not the only one using the path: heart-shaped deer tracks are impressed in the soft dirt. Just as I note the tracks, there's a loud crash over my right shoulder. I turn in time to see a doe bound away through the woods.

Before long, I sit down on a fallen log to undertake blister maintenance. While I apply moleskin to my toe, I study a black ant purposefully pushing a

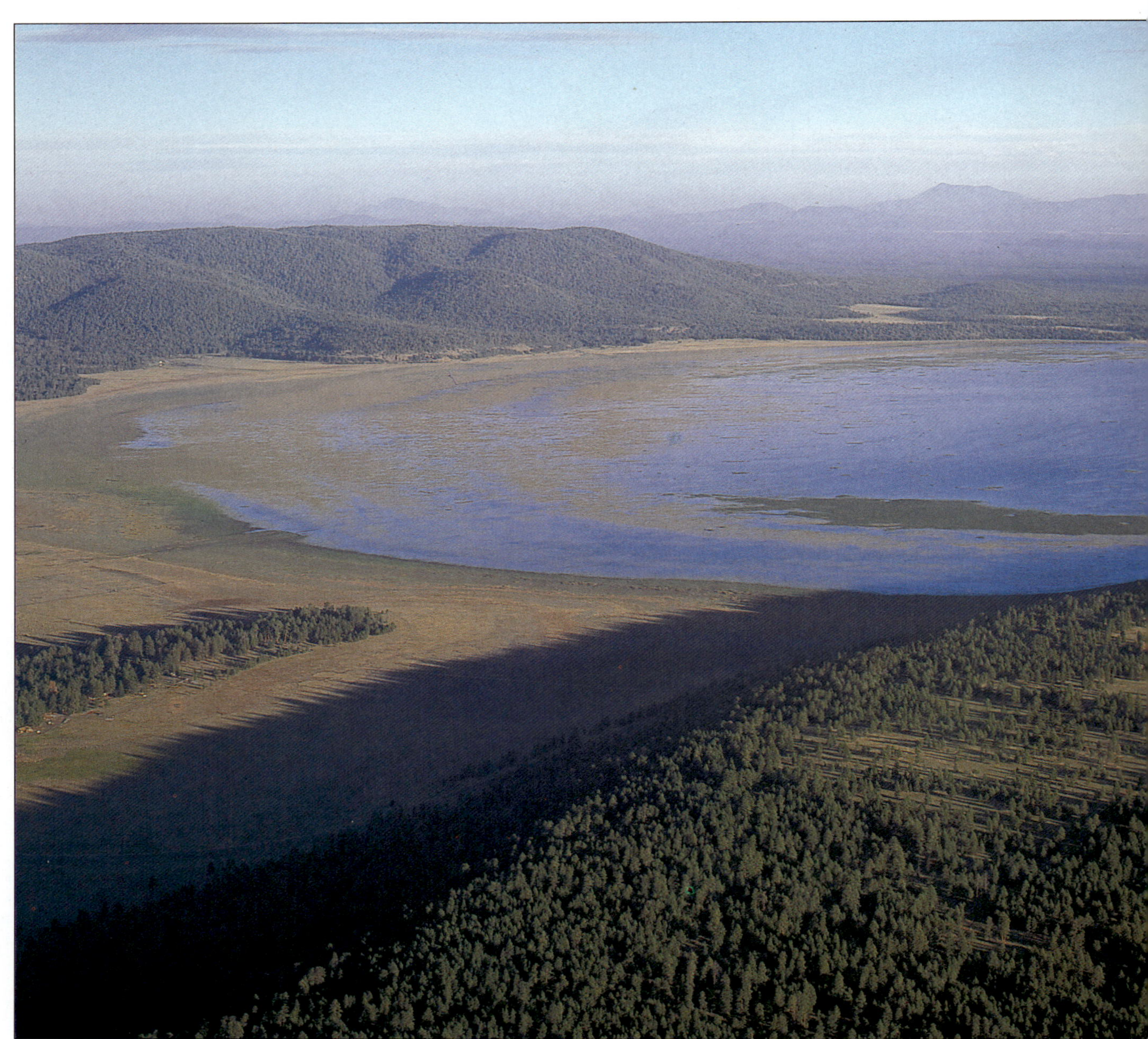

fir needle into the decaying wood at the base of my log chair.

This pause is well-timed. Watching the ant, I start to feel myself adjusting to the pace of the forest. For me, it's not the summits or the destinations that are so important, but the getting there. I've never understood the question "Is it worth it?" posed by passing hikers.

Higher on the mountain, the trail flattens out, unconcerned with getting anywhere fast. I walk amid groves of aspen and big fir and spruce trees. Some huge stumps reveal bygone logging days. Flickers and juncos flash through the branches. The summer has been so dry that most wildflowers have already finished blooming, and their leaves and stalks are turning into golden husks.

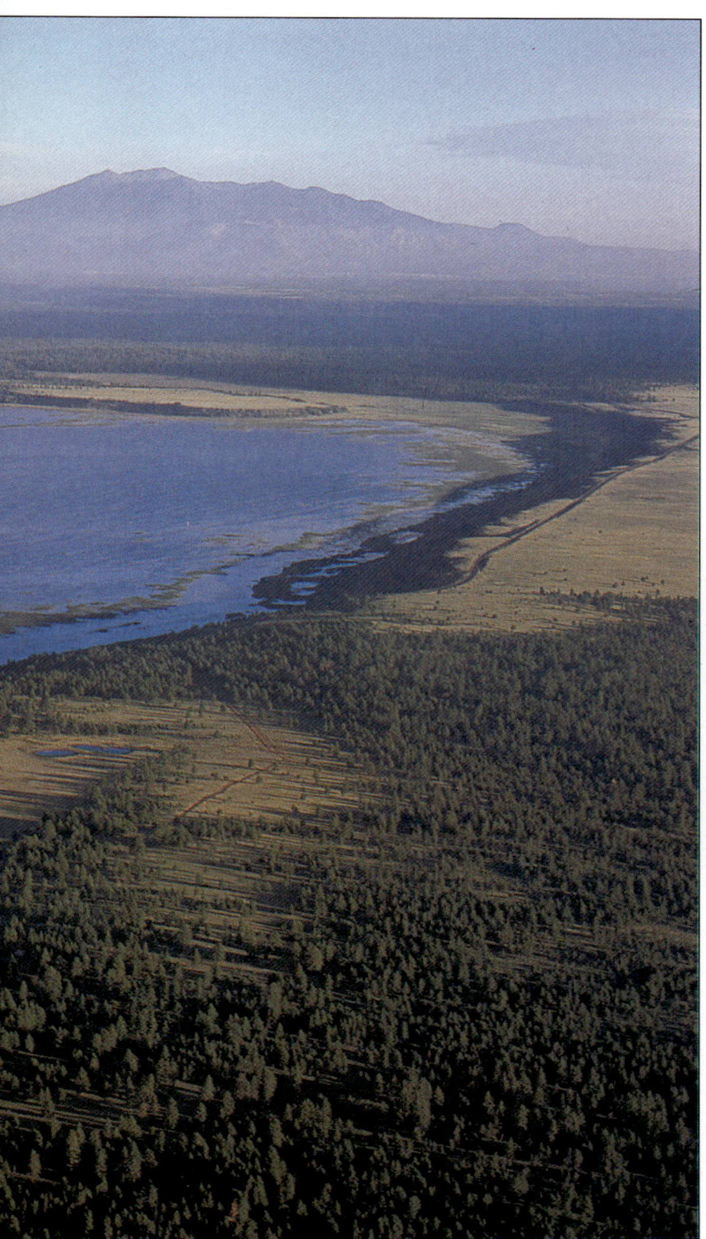

I reach a dirt road that apparently continues on to transmitter towers — a destination not nearly as inviting as sitting under the cool shade of an aspen, sipping water, and partaking of a midmorning snack.

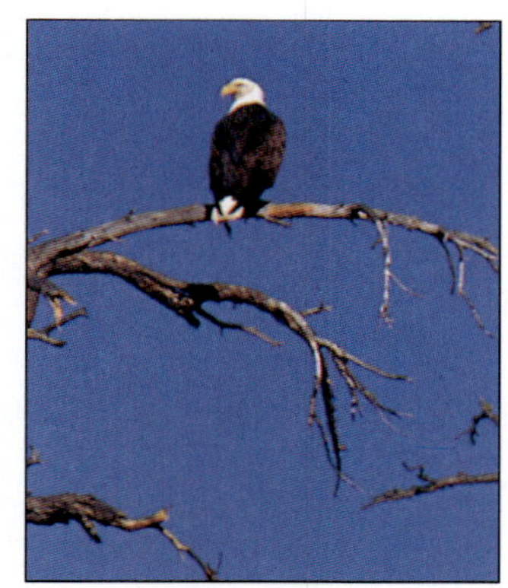

As I start for home around noon, dark thunderheads have built up nicely over the San Francisco Peaks. The clouds are a welcome sight, a sign that the monsoon season, late this year, may finally have arrived.

Getting there: Drive southeast from Flagstaff on Lake Mary Road (Forest Highway 3) about 20 miles and turn right onto Mormon Lake Road (FR 90). Drive another three miles to Dairy Springs Amphitheater. Watch for the sign that says Mormon Mountain and Ledges trails. Turn right at the sign and drive the short distance to the trailhead.

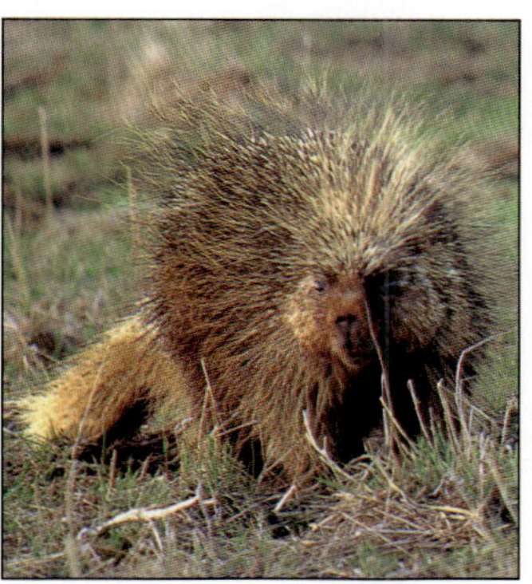

(TOP) *A bald eagle, the most impressive fisherman of Flagstaff's lake country, perches on a snag.*
FRANK ZULLO
(ABOVE) *A prickly porcupine pretty much gets it own way wherever it chooses to go.*
BILL GOBUS
(LEFT FOREGROUND) *From the top of Mormon Mountain, hikers are rewarded with vistas of Mormon Lake and the San Francisco Peaks to the north.*
MICHAEL COLLIER

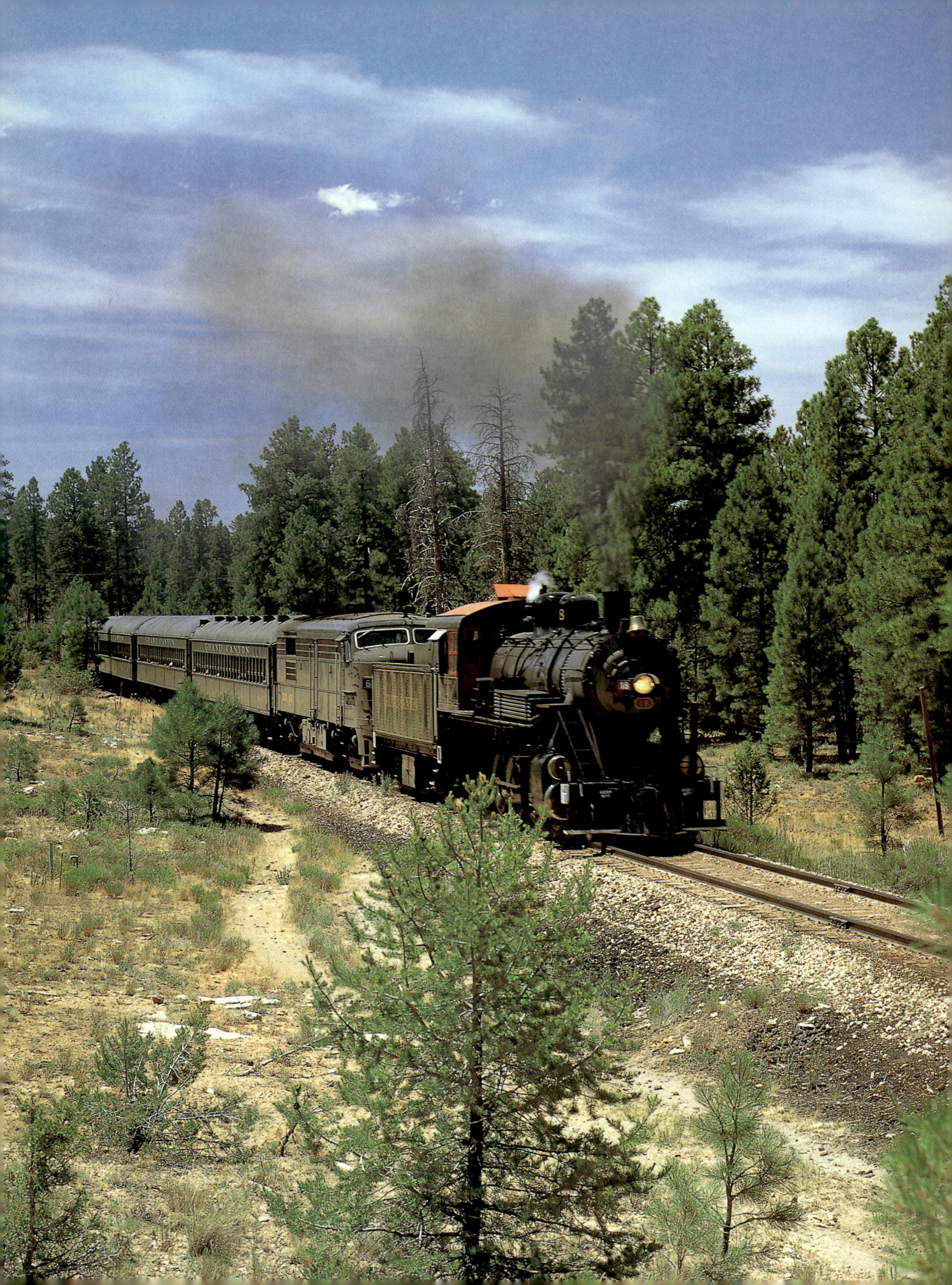
GRAND CANYON

Chapter Five

West of the Peaks

Williams, the Grand Canyon Railway, and the Kaibab National Forest

Aaaall aboard, called the conductor at the Williams train station, 32 miles west of Flagstaff. I climbed into an olive-green Harriman coach on the Number 2 northbound train, the *Williams Flyer*, headed for the Grand Canyon. Taking my seat, I noticed the old coaches have been tastefully restored, complete with green velvet seats, green window shades, and wood trim. Outside on the boarding platform, Two Feathers and his Wily Wild West Show finished entertaining, leaving the waiting passengers laughing; and finally, everyone started boarding the train. After finding their seats, some passengers reached for blankets on the overhead rack to ward off the chill until the heaters warmed the cars.

The steam engine's melodic whistle heralded our departure, and, huffing and chuffing, the train pulled out of the rail yard. At the crossings, people got out of their cars to wave at us.

Bobby, the friendly, young coach attendant, came by with a big basket of crackers and Cokes in bottles with red straws. I asked him if he liked his job. "Sure," he said. "How many 21-year-olds can say they've worked on the steam train to Grand Canyon."

The fortunes of the town of Williams have in part been tied to railroads almost since its beginnings in 1879 when Charles Thomas Rogers settled at the base of Bill Williams Mountain. Rogers' ranch became the town's first post office on June 14, 1881, with Rogers as postmaster.

Other homesteaders found the cool climate especially suited to farming potatoes, and at the end of the summer of 1881, the local newspaper reported that Mr. J.F. Scott's potato "trees" were looking well. In that same year, in anticipation of the coming of the Atlantic & Pacific Railroad, another important Williams industry, lumber, began when the Wilson & Haskell Sawmill started operations.

The A&P tracks arrived in Williams on September 1, 1882. By then, the town's business district consisted of Railroad Avenue, known as "Saloon Row," for the various establishments that catered to the cowboys, loggers, and railroad workers who came in to slake

(OPPOSITE PAGE) *The sights and sounds of the steam train era come to life once again as the resurrected Grand Canyon Railway carries visitors from Williams to the South Rim of the Grand Canyon.* BOB AND SUZANNE CLEMENZ
(FOLLOWING PANEL, PAGES 54-55) *The wilds of the Sycamore Canyon Wilderness south of Williams mark the dramatic southern edge of the high country of northern Arizona.* DICK DIETRICH

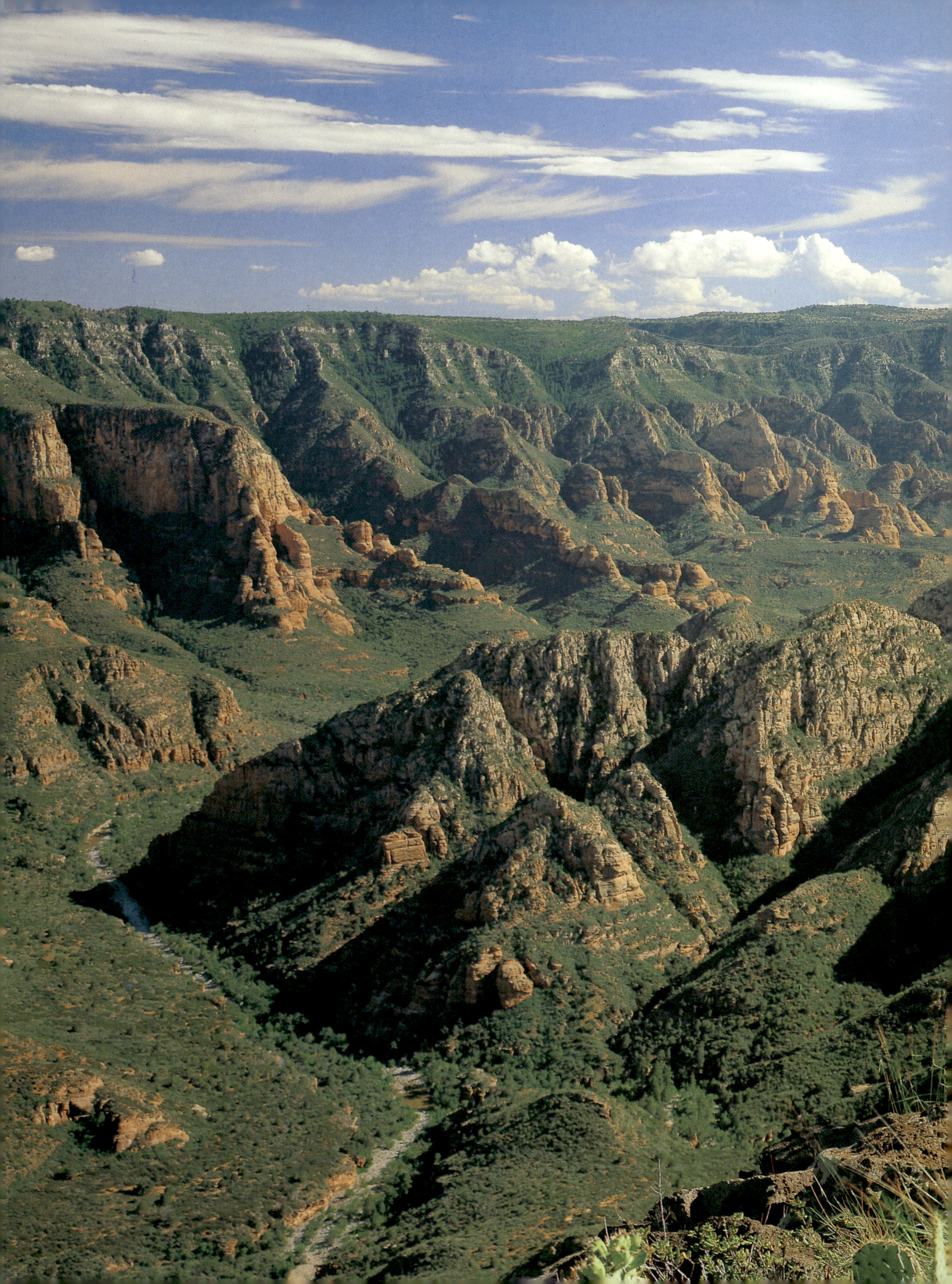

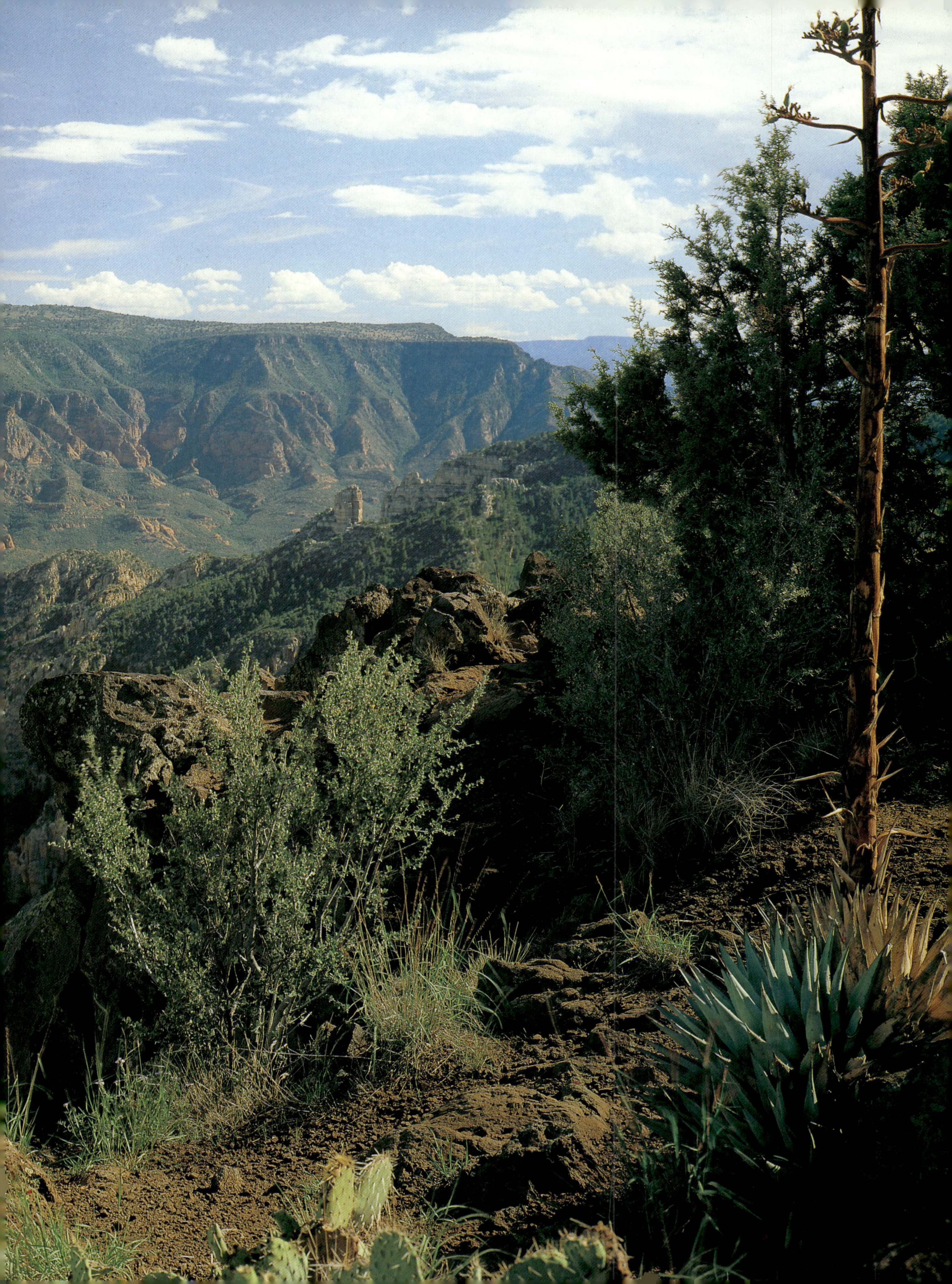

their thirsts. Paralleling it, Bill Williams Avenue was home to more respectable businesses.

In 1900, a spur was built off the main rail line at Williams to serve mines to the north. Though the mining ventures failed, the Santa Fe Railway, which had purchased the A&P, completed the 60-mile-long Grand Canyon Railway to the South Rim in the autumn of 1901, and Williams became a tourist hub. Travelers could buy a ticket on the steam train out of Williams for $3.95. Over the next 67 years the Grand Canyon Railway carried millions of passengers from Williams, confirming the town's claim to fame as the "Gateway to the Grand Canyon."

In 1968, the Grand Canyon Railway shut down operations due to financial difficulties. It was a blow to Williams, which was already in the doldrums from the closure of other industries: the Santa Fe main rail line had withdrawn its Williams base, the area's sawmills and box factory had closed, and there was talk of an interstate bypass around the town.

News of the freeway "scared Williams to death," said local resident Bob Dean.

The completion of Interstate 40 around Williams came to pass in 1984. But by 1989, things began looking up for the town. Private investors had financed a restoration of the Grand Canyon Railway, a real shot in the arm for Williams. Tourists — most of them Grand Canyon bound — now exit the interstate, fill their coolers with ice, buy food, spend the night and board the train in the morning.

Spruced up gift shops, antique stores, art galleries, restaurants, a host of motels, bed and breakfasts, barber shops, liquor stores, ice cream parlors, the venerable Grand Canyon Hotel, and the famous Sultana Bar and Theater line Bill Williams Avenue.

For Bob Dean and other Williams natives, it's land and family that brought and hold them here. Dean's grandparents and great-grandparents homesteaded at Government Prairie, northeast of town. His grandparents also owned a grocery store in Williams — Pop and Mom Marion's was the name.

As a youngster, Bob spent all his extra time on his great-uncle's ranch just north of Kendrick Mountain. As he got older he cowboyed for other ranchers in the area. Growing up in Williams, Bob recalls, meant the sounds of the trains, and many days spent fishing on the nearby lakes. Dogtown Reservoir is his favorite.

As he started a family, Dean switched from cowboying to highway construction and contracting, and finally ended up in real estate. He thought it would be a "good way to wake up in the same county every morning." Besides, says Dean, "I know the country." Now he sells five-acre ranches to the many Californian immigrants to northern Arizona. "It took a long time before I could get used to calling five acres a ranch," he remarked in his droll manner.

Hanging behind Dean's desk at Poquette Real Estate on Bill Williams Avenue are his black cowboy hat and a wonderful pencil illustration of him with his wife's horse. His eyes light up when he tells about his father, Denton "Diz" Dean, helping to found the Bill Williams Mountain Men, who dress in buckskins and ride

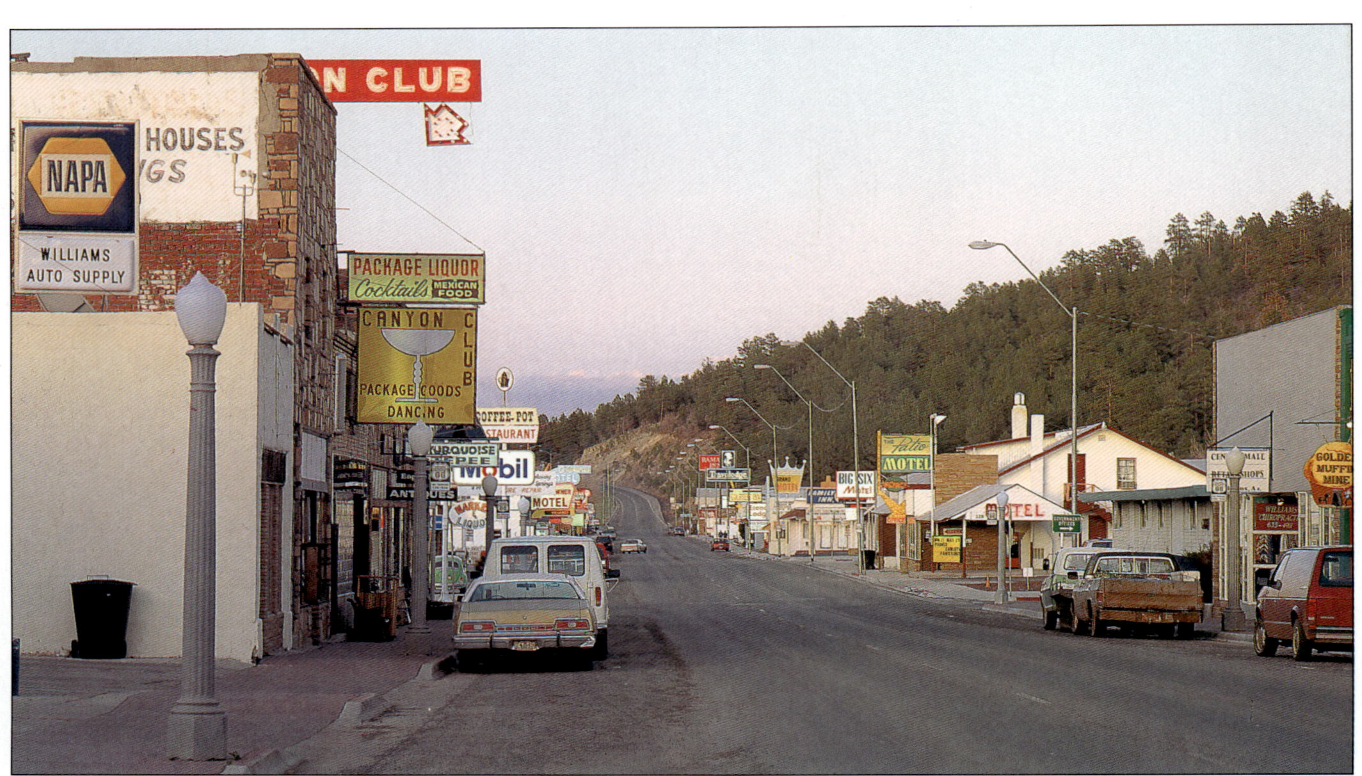

horseback in parades, including five presidential inaugurations in Washington, D.C. The big event for the mountain men is their weeklong winter ride each year from Williams to Phoenix and back. Bob's done 30 rides (more than 6,000 miles, and he's aiming for 50). "I've been through a lot of horses," he laughs.

A former rodeo bareback and bull rider, Dean has also worked to bring back the Labor Day Pro Rodeo to Williams. Such efforts fit with the town's attempts to make Williams more of a destination for tourists. Dean would like to see some growth in the town — perhaps doubling its present population of about 2,500 bringing the town near its peak of the 1940s and '50s. He also wants light industry providing jobs so the town's children won't have to move away when they grow up.

Will he always stay in Williams? So far, says Bob Dean, "I haven't found any place I like better."

To the south of Williams' two main drags, neighborhoods of neat, unassuming houses line tree-shaded streets. Homes like the yellow bungalow on Grant Avenue that belongs to Don and Kathryn Massey. I found them out in their garden, trimming wild rose bushes — Kathryn in a sunbonnet, Don in suspenders.

Don Massey is nearly a native of Williams. He came to town in 1919, from Vernal, Utah. His father, Ira Massey, was a veterinarian "who liked pine trees" and decided to settle here, Don Massey said. Kathryn Massey was a Harvey Girl, and Don became chief of police in Williams. "I just stumbled into it, said I'd do it one day and one night," Don Massey recalled. He stayed in the job 25 years.

His predecessor had been shot and killed in a fracas in the Sultana Bar. With that history, Kathryn Massey admitted she was concerned about her husband's choice of occupation. "I thought sure he'd get killed," she said.

"Everybody had a gun in those days. It was just a way of life," Don Massey observed.

Now the two, in their mid-80s, are retired. Their son lives next door, and their lives are much calmer. Though they've traveled a great deal, they always return to Williams. "We're stuck here now," Kathryn Massey chuckled. But it doesn't look like a bad life — their vegetable garden is thriving, their house is surrounded by splendid hollyhocks, and a big yellow tomcat, her "tramp kitty," appears well fed and content.

Not everyone in Williams can trace their family histories back as far as Bob Dean or Don and Kathryn Massey. Mayor Calder Chapman came here only 20 years ago and knows that he's still considered an outsider.

I found him at his business on Bill Williams Avenue, the local Radio Shack. A retired hospital administrator from Southern California, Chapman is the town's first elected mayor. (They'd been appointed previously.) Now serving his second term, Chapman likes the job — "the fun part is cutting ribbons"— and he likes the town. "Hey, I like everything about Williams — the pine trees, we've got some awful nice people here, and the surroundings especially the Grand Canyon." One thing he wishes Williams had is a movie theater, but he's been twice to see the local stage production of *Godspell* at the Sultana.

His vision for Williams? "Increase the quality of life. It's trite . . . but we need to get some diversity and good-paying jobs." The biggest immediate goal is to attract new industry, but the mayor is adamant that it must be low- or no-water using.

Back on the Grand Canyon train, we moved along at a steady clip of 30 to 35 miles an hour crossing Cataract Creek and passing Pitt, Red Lake, and Quivero stations. The landscape changed dramatically as the tracks descended from the ponderosa forest around Williams into piñon-juniper and open grass and shrub terrain — good cow country. Several corrals and chutes beside the tracks signaled points where livestock were loaded onto the train in the old days. Guitar- and banjo-strumming musicians strolled from car to car entertaining us with cowboy and folk songs.

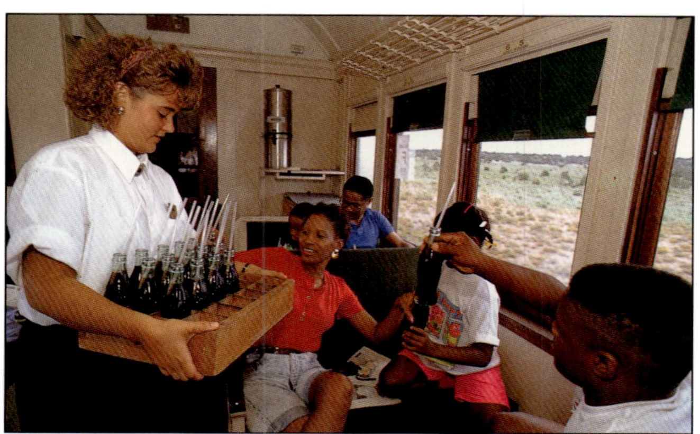

(OPPOSITE PAGE AND LEFT) *Though Interstate 40 passed it by, Williams is enjoying the benefits of the resurgence of interest in Old Route 66.*
MICHAEL COLLIER
(ABOVE) *Passengers on the Grand Canyon Railway quench their thirsts during the ride to the Grand Canyon.*
CHRISTINE KEITH

At the small town of Valle, the train started climbing, winding through Coconino Canyon and heading up a four-percent grade to the South Rim of the Grand Canyon at 6,850 feet. At our leisurely speed, the trip to the Canyon typically takes two and a half hours, but our journey stretched into three and a half hours when a wheel bearing on the car in front of us overheated. The train had to back down to the Apex siding, uncouple the ailing car, and leave it there. Our car was reattached and we were on our way again. Just another adventure of train travel circa 1901.

Soon the train pulled into the Grand Canyon Railway Station, a restored log building built about 1910, located across from the famous El Tovar Hotel. For the next three and half hours, we were free to lunch at one of the restaurants on the South Rim, walk the West Rim path, or ride a tour bus for more sightseeing. Sated with views of the magnificent Grand Canyon (if that's possible), we reboarded the train and headed back to Williams. Rootin'- tootin' gunfighters staging a train robbery livened up the trip home.

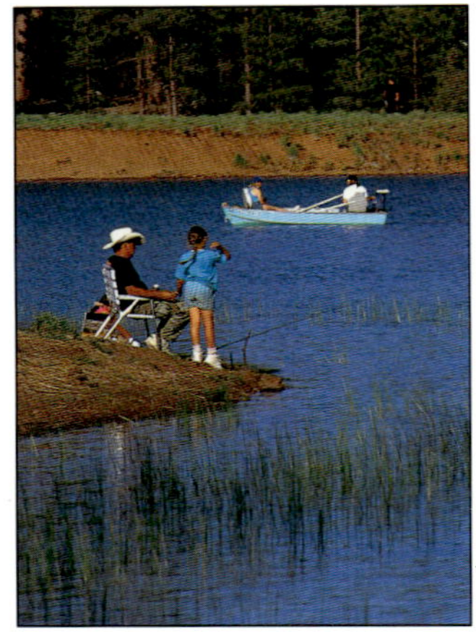

The South Kaibab National Forest, originally called the Tusayan National Forest, surrounds Williams. The forest was established in 1910, with headquarters in the town. The Forest Service has remained an important presence in Williams, both for the employment it provides and for the beautiful land it administers.

In 1923, young Clyde Moose came from Texas to Williams. He'd passed the forest ranger exam, his life's dream, and was ready to tackle his new assignment. In those days, forest rangers did a little bit of everything — counted livestock on the range, marked trees for timber sales, rounded up wild horses, put in fences and telephone lines, and fought fires.

In his first year as a ranger, Clyde built the wooden fire lookout tower on top of Bill Williams Mountain. Every Monday he would hike the six miles from his house to the tower and be on the job at 8 a.m. He'd camp in a tent on top of the mountain through the week, and hike home each Saturday night.

Clyde became district ranger on the 250,000-acre Chalender District on the "Old Kaibab." He and his wife, Ruby, got around like all their neighbors did, mostly on horseback, snowshoes, or skis. At their home 10 miles east of Williams, they cooked and heated with wood, as winter temperatures occasionally reached -20 degrees F.

The South Kaibab is a big forest with plenty to explore — several high peaks including Bill Williams Mountain, lovely trout-filled lakes, a spectacular canyon overlook, old Route 66, and more.

The lakes surrounding Williams were built to supply the town with water, and they double as popular recreational spots. North of town are Cataract and Kaibab lakes. Cataract Lake, about a mile northwest of Williams on Cataract Lake Road, is open mid-May to the end of October. It covers 45 acres and offers an 18-unit campground, fishing, boating, picnicking, and hiking. Kaibab Lake, just off State Route 64 to the Grand Canyon, is 65 acres with a large campground and interpretive programs in the summer.

South of Williams are, in order, Dogtown Reservoir, White Horse, and JD Dam lakes. To find them, take South Fourth Street out of town. It becomes the Perkinsville Road (Forest Road 173). To reach Dogtown Reservoir, drive about 3.5 miles, then turn east (left) on FR 140. Another three miles takes you to FR 132, three-quarters of a mile farther and you're at the 60-site campground and boat ramp. Check out the three-quarter-mile nature trail down Dogtown Wash and the 1.8-mile trail around the lake.

White Horse Lake has the most amenities of the lakes around Williams — roomy campground, boat rentals, a dock, cabins, and a store. To reach White Horse, again take the Perkinsville Road out of Williams this time for nine miles and turn left (east)

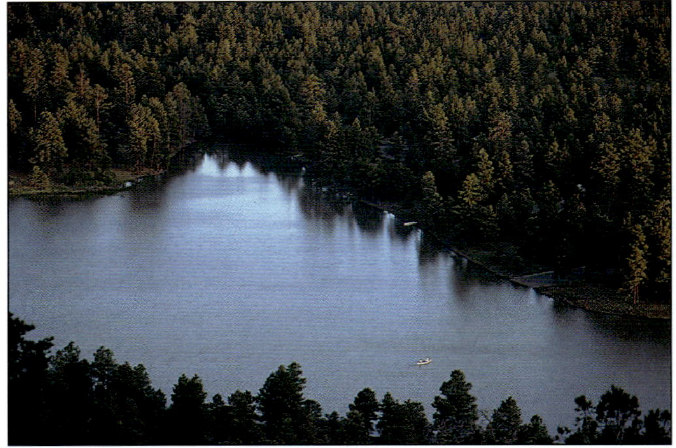

(ABOVE, LEFT) *White Horse Lake east of Williams is one of the most popular summertime destinations for visitors and locals alike.* MICHAEL COLLIER
(ABOVE) *Tiny Kaibab Lake, just north of town, is another fine camping and fishing spot.* INGE MARTIN

on White Horse Lake Road (FR 110) for six miles. Turn left again at Forest Road 109 for another three miles to the lake.

To find JD Dam Lake, continue on White Horse Lake Road (FR 110) another three miles southeast until you turn right on FR 105. JD Dam Lake, named for 19th-century rancher James Douglas, is small. Fishing there is restricted to artificial lures and flies only; no bait. The smart brown trout the lake is stocked with make fishing JD challenging.

Sycamore Point lies still another five miles farther southeast on Forest Road 110. Visitors stand in awe before this precipitous drop-off overlooking the Sycamore Canyon Wilderness. This rocky defile, which has been called "little Grand Canyon," is a spectacularly beautiful, wild, and rugged wilderness, and a prime black bear habitat. There are a few undeveloped campsites at Sycamore Point, but there is no access into the canyon there.

Bill Williams Mountain is a big-shouldered, forested, volcanic peak that rises south of the town of Williams. It's a quiet place where you can camp in a grove of big ponderosas and see them bathed in the light of a three-quarter moon.

The mountain was named for legendary mountain man William Sherley Williams in 1851 by the Sitgreaves Expedition. His name also graces the Bill Williams River in western Arizona, and the Bill Williams Fork, a tributary of the river. Williams, known by fellow mountain men as "Old Bill," was born January 3, 1787, and was raised with his eight siblings on a Missouri farm. He became a circuit preacher and missionary among his boyhood friends, the Osage Indians. But the missionary became the convert and Williams married an Osage woman, eventually becoming "more Indian than the Indians." After the death of his wife he headed west and took up trapping. His knowledge of the country and the Indians led him to work as a guide and translator on the 1825 U.S. government survey of the Santa Fe Trail.

He wandered throughout the West and trapped along Arizona's Gila River in October 1826. In 1837 he met Antoine Leroux while trapping in northern Arizona and they became fast friends. It was Leroux who suggested Williams' name for the mountain while Leroux was guiding the Sitgreaves Expedition. Old Bill Williams never saw his name on a map for he was killed by Ute Indians in Colorado on March 14, 1849.

Driving the winding seven-mile gravel Forest Road 111 off the Perkinsville Road to the 9,256-foot summit on a late spring afternoon, we passed thick stands of aspen and oak and huge firs. Purple lupine and currant bushes were in bloom. Atop Bill Williams Mountain we found Kris Magill and her Chihuahua, Happy, who keeps her company in the fire lookout

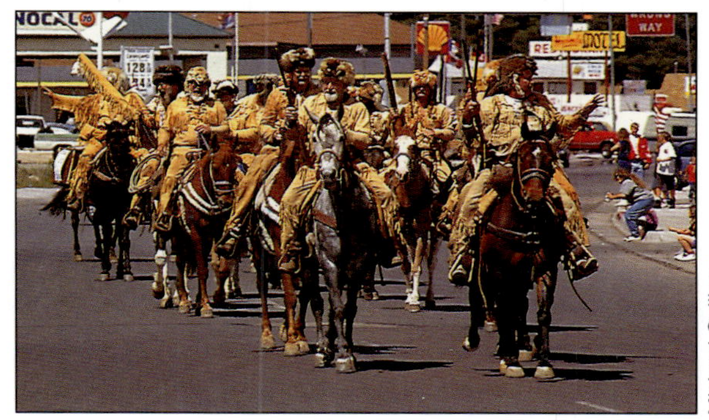
Michael Collier

Williams Rendezvous Days

An authentic buckskinner is a person who apologizes if he has to use a match. For him, it is a point of honor to be able to start a fire with a flint, not to mention set a trap, shoot a black-powder rifle, and find his way through the woods. All are antique skills that uphold the spirit of old mountain man Bill Williams.

In a reliving of that tradition, the buckskinners gather in Williams each Memorial Day weekend for Rendezvous Days. They pitch canvas teepees in the shade of the pines in Buckskinner Park just south of town, sharing a hefty dose of fellowship with like-minded folk. A good bit of tall-tale swapping goes on, and down Traders Row you can view and buy a fur hat, a well-seasoned Dutch oven, or a handsewn rawhide dress.

Down at the shooting range, buckskinner Steve Danish, an electrician in real life, showed me how to load a black-powder rifle. "The powder, patch, and ball technique is the way you load it," he stressed. "Any other way is wrong." Steve measured out the grains of black powder into a hollowed out piece of antler (his is a 38-grain; a hunting load runs about 100 grains).

Then you pour in the powder, put a small patch of pillow ticking over the end of the barrel, trim the patch, and place a lead ball on top. This neat little bundle is driven tightly down into the gun barrel with a ramrod. A hunter must be a good stalker because the range of a black-powder flintlock rifle is only about 75 yards.

For Steve Danish, the purpose of all this is not to get a deer each autumn. For him, it's deeper than that: It's "our heritage, where our freedom came from," he declared.

Rendezvous Days begin Saturday morning with a parade down Bill Williams Avenue (Old Route 66). There's also food, crafts, dances, and music during the weekend.

tower. The lookout, which becomes crowded with three people inside, is dominated by the alidade that sits smack in the middle of the small room. Kris showed us how she pinpoints the location of "smokes" through the crosshairs of the surveying instrument. While there haven't been any big fires on the forest in several years, there have been many smaller ones. Sycamore Canyon to the south is especially prone to lightning strikes, she said. And as the highest point for miles around, Kris is in a vulnerable location herself. But after 30 years she has experienced only one strike close enough to leave her shaken for several minutes.

A Trail to Prehistoric Times

Where there was water, there were people. A place called Keyhole Sink well proves this maxim of the Southwest. Hidden in this inconspicuous box canyon is a pool, and with it are rock drawings that hint at the importance of this place to prehistoric people.

It's an easy walk to Keyhole Sink, barely a mile over fairly level ground through open forest. As you approach the "sink," though, the scene begins to change. You come into the midst of a cool grove of aspen saplings, the ground is moist, and a basalt cliff rises around you.

Survey the cliffs above the pool and you'll soon notice a panel of pictures pecked into the basalt. One scene depicts deer coming into a keyhole-shaped canyon to drink water. If you were a hunter in prehistoric times, you would have considered this a good place to ambush game animals. Wildlife still make frequent visits here.

To reach Keyhole Sink, travel east from Williams on I-40 to the Pittman Valley exit. Turn left, cross the interstate, and head east on Old Route 66 for about two miles to the Oak Hill Snowplay area. Park here and go directly across the road to the green gate. This is the trailhead. Watch for the blue triangle blazes on trees along the trail. (They mark the way for cross-country skiers in winter.)

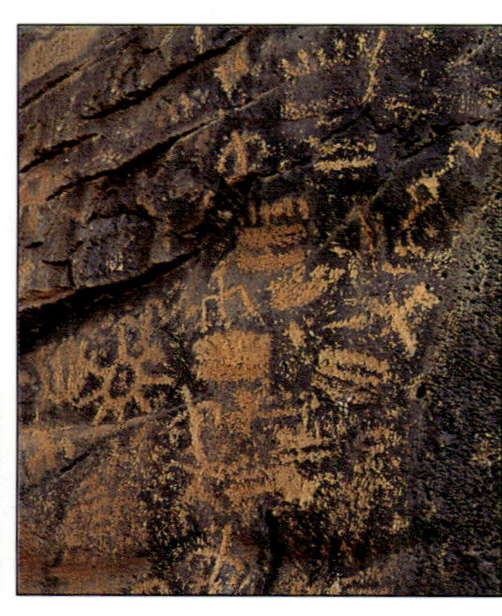

Stewart Aitchison

Kris Magill's life as a lookout today is a far cry from her days as a white-stockinged Harvey Girl. When she was 18, Kris worked as a waitress at the Harvey House in Williams. But then she got married, "which was more interesting," she said. Her husband launched her on a new career — as a fire lookout on top of Bill Williams Mountain. The first time she climbed the steps up the 60-foot-high tower, Kris told a local reporter, was the last time she wore a dress to work.

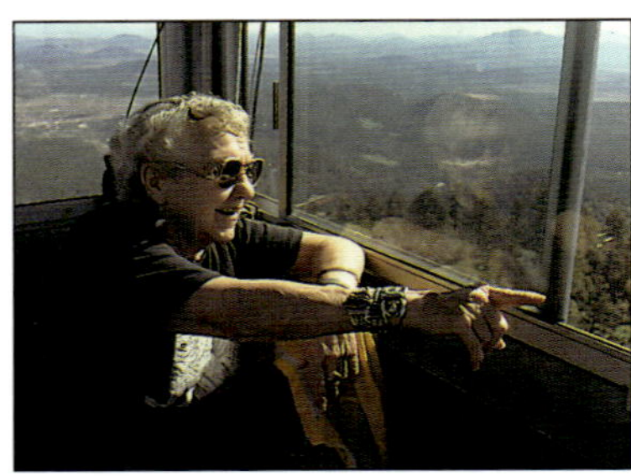

From her tower aerie Kris Magill enjoys a magnificent 360-degree view of the Coconino Plateau and the Kaibab National Forest. She points out the North Rim of the Grand Canyon, Mount Trumbull (nearly in Utah), and the San Francisco Peaks. Turning south, she looks at Sycamore Canyon and Mingus Mountain and every lake and cinder hill in between. She knows too, mostly by their voices on the radio, all the other men and women who keep vigil in surrounding forest lookouts.

You also can hike up the mountain. One route, the Bill Williams Trail, built in 1902, starts from the Forest Service's Williams District Office. Along the way a coyote may cross the trail, and in May clumps of wild iris and bright pink phlox brighten the forest floor. On warm mornings, chickadees call from the trees, and the air is redolent with the vanilla smell of ponderosa pine.

Some people travel to Bill Williams Mountain for the downhill ski slope. Located on the north side of the mountain, the "family-style" Williams Ski Area offers four runs served by a poma lift and a rope tow. The slopes are suitable for beginner, intermediate, and advanced skiers. A small lodge at the base serves hot food. Generally, if snow conditions are adequate, the ski area opens in mid-December. From Williams, turn south on Fourth Street, go 2.5 miles to FR106; turn right and follow it to the ski area. The cinder-surfaced road is plowed when the ski area is open.

Williams made history in 1984 as the last Route 66 town bypassed by Interstate 40. The local historic preservation committee decided to sell chunks of concrete from Old 66 at $4.66 apiece. Teri Cleeland, Kaibab Forest historian and tracer of old routes and trails, was amazed at the response. Friends from as far away as New England, she said, called her after seeing

(ABOVE) *Kris Magill watches for fires.* MICHAEL COLLIER
(OPPOSITE PAGE) *The Coconino Plateau lies between the Bill Williams fire tower, and the San Francisco Peaks on the horizon.* BOB AND SUZANNE CLEMENZ

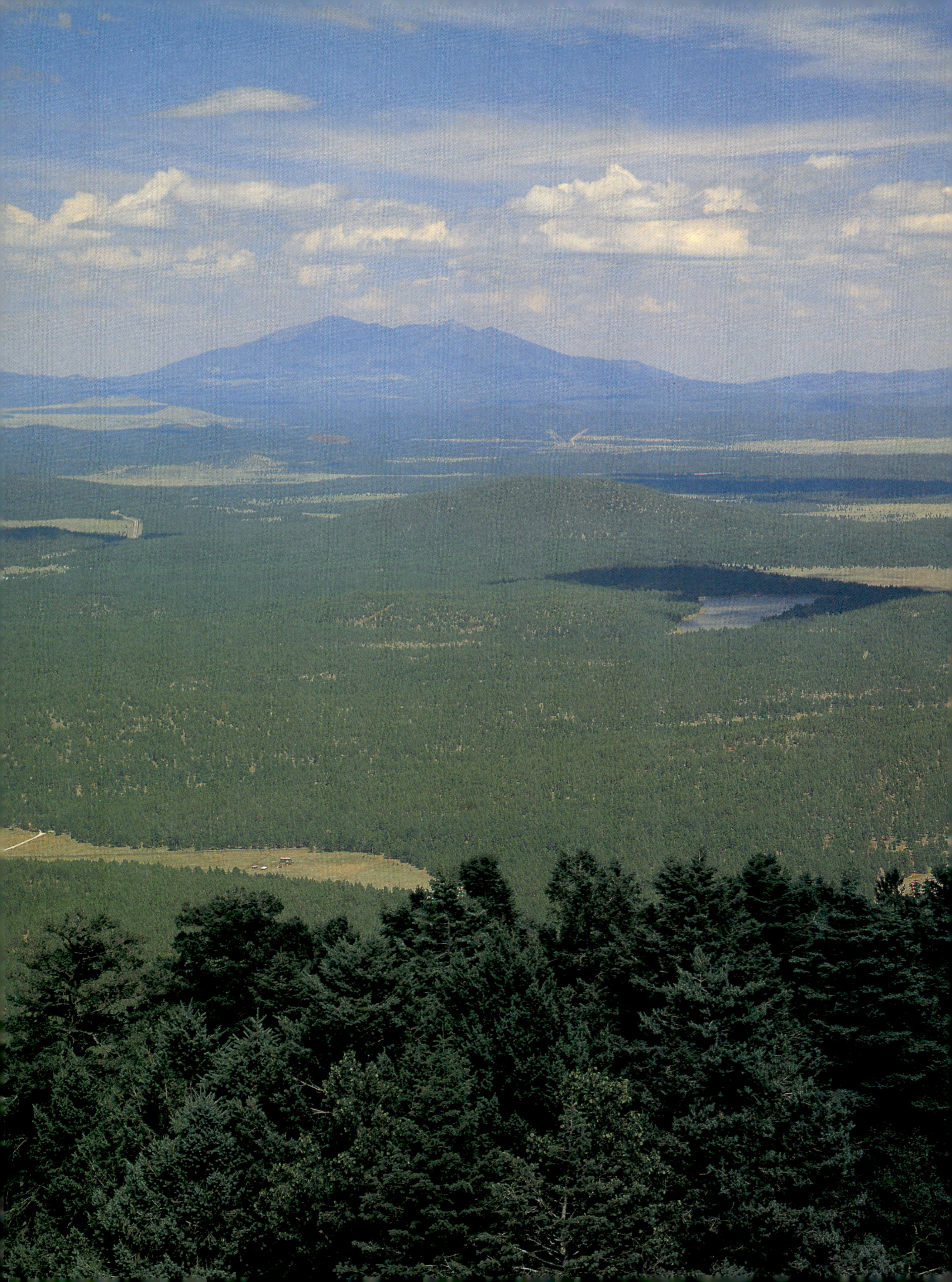

stories in the national press. The $5,000 raised went toward renovating the Santa Fe freight depot as the town's new visitor center.

All over the country, a wave of Route 66 nostalgia has curled over people. We remember the songs, TV shows, and fine old Chevys — it was a time, many of us want to believe, that was somehow simpler and maybe better, when you could spend the night in a concrete wigwam, quaff some cold cider by the roadside, and have your oil checked by a friendly service station attendant.

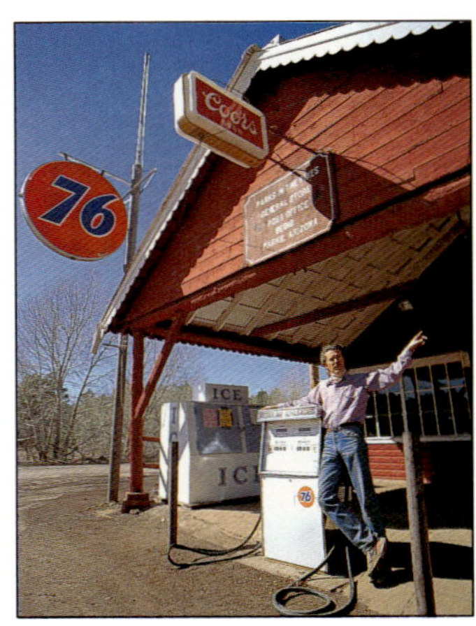

Scott Baxter at Parks in the Pines General Store.
MICHAEL COLLIER

Some classic Route 66 hotels and dining spots can still be found in Williams. Marshall Duncan's Highlander Motel sits along Old Route 66 (Bill Williams Avenue). A 50-year resident of Williams, Mr. Duncan remembers when there were only stop signs along the route, and traffic would be backed up for blocks. Williams hasn't changed much, Marshall says, and people haven't either, really. The only change he's noticed is, they aren't as frugal as they used to be. But they're still "just nice people."

Old Smoky's Pancake House serves up incredible homemade breads, and Rod's Steak House is located just up the street. The late Rodney Graves, with his wife, Helen, came to Williams during the World War II years and built and operated the restaurant until 1967. One of his dishwashers, Lawrence Sanchez, now runs it with his wife, Stella. Lawrence came out and visited with us one evening as we ate our dinner. He said he'd left Williams briefly as a young man, but found he never really wanted to live anywhere else.

Route 66 nostalgia grabbed me one day, as my husband and I headed home from Williams to Flagstaff. The map showed a stretch of Old Route 66 paralleling new Interstate 40. The mystique of the road was too much to pass up. Besides, if you want to get somewhere fast, you take the interstate. But if you want to feel the country and meet the people, you take back roads at any opportunity.

We took I-40 east out of Williams, exited at Pittman Valley Road, headed north over the interstate, and turned right (east) onto Route 66. The rutted and patched two-lane asphalt, no doubt a few years older than I am, saunters through pine forest and grassy meadows, past country stores, abandoned gas stations and motels, and old homesteads. Beside the road, blue Auto Tour signs relay history and show various alternate routes the road has taken through its life.

At the crossroads of Parks, you can gas up and step back in time at Parks in the Pines General Store and Post Office. In operation for more than 80 years, this red-log original is still open and hopping with customers. If he's not too busy, storekeeper Scott Baxter is happy to stop and visit. In the store, you'll find baskets of potatoes, an old wood stove, and — a sign of the times — videos for rent. The store serves as general community center for residents of Parks and Spring Valley. Just outside Parks, you can walk an abandoned gravel stretch of the road, as it was in 1931.

East of Parks, Route 66 curves north and turns into dirt for a few miles. Soon, you arrive at the lovely spot called Brannigan Park, the highest point — 7,300 feet above sea level — on the entire 2,448 miles of "America's Main Street." From Brannigan Park, you can travel another six miles to Bellemont. Then it's 10 more miles on I-40 into Flagstaff.

Williams is still the quiet side of the Peaks. Without much trouble you can find your own private campsite in the surrounding forest, hike an uncrowded trail, or locate some hungry trout. You can talk to friendly folks on the street, who, with some encouragement, may tell stories about their grandparents or great-grandparents, who arrived by covered wagon. And as background music, there's always the melodic whistle of the old steam train.

When You Go

Contact:
Williams Chamber of Commerce
820 West Bill Williams Avenue
P.O. Box 235
Williams, AZ 86046-0235
(602) 635-4061

Kaibab National Forest
Supervisor's Office
800 South 6th Street
Williams, AZ 86046
(602) 635-8200

The Williams/Forest Service Visitor Center, located in the historic Santa Fe Railroad Depot at 200 West Railroad Avenue, is open every day from 8 a.m. until 6 p.m.
Telephone (602) 635-4061.

The Cohonina

Were they a backward bunch of wanderers? Or adept hunters, well tuned to their mountain and plateau home? Archaeologists are seeking answers to these questions about a group of prehistoric people called the Cohonina.

From about A.D. 700 until 1100 these people built dwellings, farmed, and hunted in the mountains and forests of the high plateau country of west-central Arizona.

Their territory stretched from the Grand Canyon south to the broken country of Sycamore Canyon and the Mogollon Rim, and from Kingman on the west to the Wupatki-Sunset Crater area on the east. The present-day town of Williams, and the surrounding South Kaibab National Forest, are considered the heartland of the Cohonina.

The name Cohonina was adapted from the Hopi term for the Havasupai and Hualapai Indians of northern and western Arizona. Early archaeologists called the Cohonina a "culture of poverty," but excavations around Sitgreaves Mountain by a new generation are altering that view.

When Cohonina congregated, it was usually around the major mountains of the region, such as Sitgreaves and Bill Williams. Their winter homes were pithouses covered with a mud, brush, and wood material called jacal, building efforts dictated by the cold weather. In what would seem to be a contrary pattern, the Cohonina apparently headed for lower elevations in summer to the piñon-juniper forests to farm. There they grew corn and squash, and probably beans. Nature would have filled their larders, too, with nuts — acorns, piñons, and walnuts — and seeds of sunflower and yucca.

Cohonina pottery was simple, mostly gray or brown with only modest decoration. What they were best known for was their work in obsidian. Cohonina stoneworkers flaked chunks of this volcanic glass into long, tapered points with serrated edges. The presence of these points says "Cohonina were here."

Three major sources of obsidian exist in the Cohonina heartland: one is Government Mountain northeast of Williams. The clear, black obsidian from this source has been found at sites all over the Southwest. Obsidian may have been traded either as raw or worked stone. The Cohonina likely could have controlled access to the few obsidian sources, and, as Kaibab Forest archaeologist Larry Lekson said, those who controlled obsidian controlled the "gold mine" of their day.

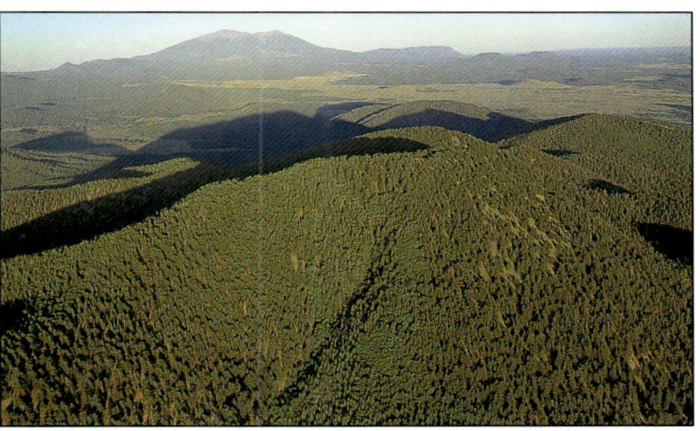

(ABOVE) *Sitgreaves Mountain was an important place to the Cohonina people who farmed and hunted in the mountain and plateau country of northern Arizona.*
(BELOW) *Forest Service volunteer Charlie Bennett entertains visitors to the Williams Ranger District Office.*
BOTH BY MICHAEL COLLIER

So it is possible the centers of the obsidian trade were the massive, high-walled rock structures the Cohonina built on top of hills. Or perhaps they served as signal stations, "safe havens" during stressful times, or territorial markers.

Clover Ruin — Hoping to uncover basic information about Cohonina dwellings, South Kaibab Forest archaeologists, with the help of volunteers, are excavating rooms of a small farmstead called the Clover Ruin. To visit it, the only Cohonina site open to the public, take Exit 161 off Interstate 40 at Williams, turn south toward town, and follow signs to the Williams District Ranger Office. The ruin is located just outside the office.

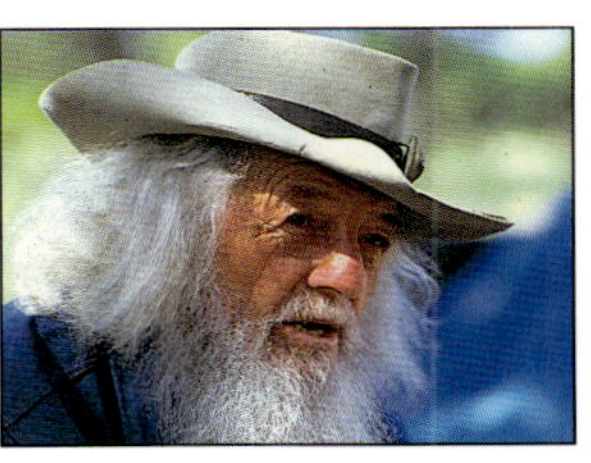

You're likely to find Charlie Bennett at the ranger office. His flowing white beard and long hair are unmistakable. For 15 summers he has been volunteering his time doing jobs for the Forest Service. But then Charlie has done nothing *but* work for most of his 75 years. He farmed for a number of years in his native Alberta, Canada, guided horse packing trips, and drove a chuck wagon at the Calgary Stampede. With only a little coaxing, Charlie will put on his special sweat-stained storytelling hat and recite one of hundreds of poems he has stored in his head, a tinge of Canada creeping into his voice.

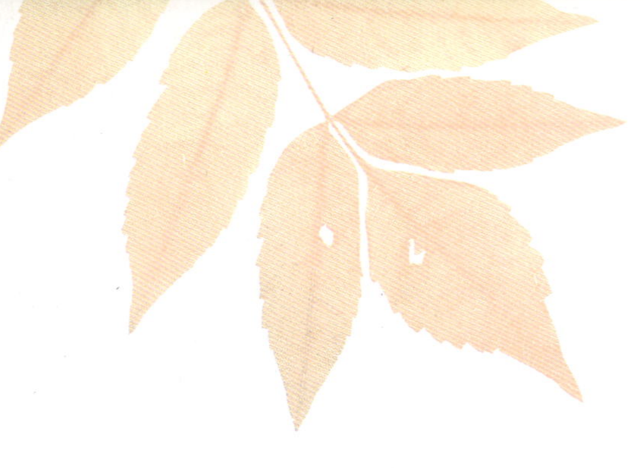

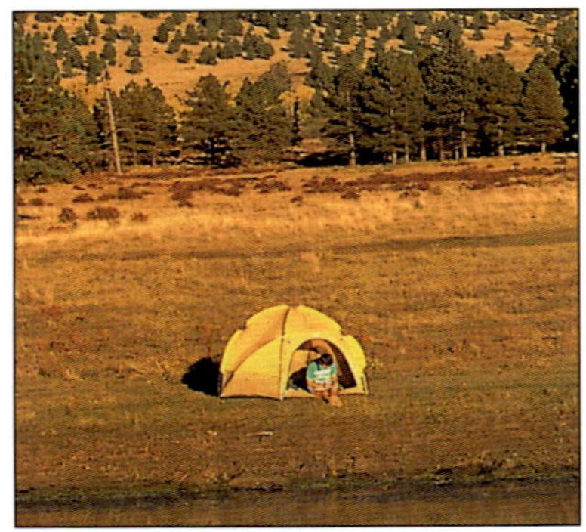

TOM BEAN

ACKNOWLEDGEMENTS

For their help with this book I would like to thank Flagstaff friends Elson Miles, Joseph and Mary Lou Vasquez, George and Sharon Yard, Richard and Sherry Mangum, Platt Cline, Joe Meehan, Billy Cordasco, and Ruth Ann Border and Dena Dierker at NAU Reprographics. In Williams, Teri Cleeland, Neil Weintraub, Bob Dean, Calder Chapman, Kris Magill, and Charlie Bennett gave generously of their time and expertise. And finally my thanks to Michael, who brought me home.

— *Rose Houk*

(INSIDE BACK COVER) *A few leaves cling to aspens in the last days of autumn.* MICHAEL COLLIER
(BACK COVER) *The Sinagua Indians lived for 600 years in Walnut Canyon east of Flagstaff.* RANDY PRENTICE